BEYOND CHECKBOXES

THE HUMAN ELEMENT OF GRC

TOLULOPE MICHAEL

TABLE OF CONTENTS

INTRODUCTION

In the ever-evolving landscape of governance, risk management, and compliance (GRC), the pursuit of robust security and adherence to intricate regulatory frameworks has been a hallmark of responsible corporate citizenship. Organizations, regardless of their size, industry, or global reach, have meticulously scrutinized, audited, and fine-tuned their systems, protocols, and policies, all with the purpose of shielding their data, assets, and reputation. The proverbial checkboxes have proliferated, multiplied, and become emblematic of an unyielding commitment to GRC, manifesting as ever-lengthening to-do lists and digital fortresses fortified with increasingly sophisticated technology.

Yet, for all the checkboxes checked and all the measures taken, the realm of GRC remains a challenging battleground. In this arena, adversaries are not bound by any code of honor or constrained by rules; they are agile, resourceful, and unceasing in their pursuit of vulnerabilities. Threats in the form of cyberattacks, data breaches, and compliance missteps continue to loom large over every organization. And they are not deterred by the tick marks and Xs on those well-frequented checklists.

The traditional approach to GRC, with its focus on technology, processes, and legal compliance, is essential. It ensures that an organization adheres to best practices, aligns with legal requirements, and maintains an organized structure for handling data and risks. But, as the digital world evolves, a new paradigm emerges: the realization that the human factor, the most enigmatic, unpredictable, and ultimately the most potent element in this complex equation, must not be underestimated.

In "Beyond Checkboxes: The Human Element of GRC," we embark on a profound exploration of this uncharted dimension of GRC. We journey into the intricate interplay between people and protocols, between human psychology and the machinery of compliance. Here, the essence of cybersecurity is not found solely within the confines of code or firewalls, but rather within the individuals who form the lifeblood of an organization. The human element, often referred to as the "human firewall," is the fulcrum upon which the organization's success or failure balances.

In an age where data is both the fuel and currency of organizations, trust is a fragile but invaluable commodity. The human element serves as both the guardian and the potential Achilles' heel in this equation. It is the factor that determines whether the fortress remains secure or becomes vulnerable, and it is this concept of the "human firewall" that lies at the heart of our exploration.

This book is a voyage of discovery, delving into the intricacies of human vulnerabilities, the psychology behind them, and the myriad challenges and solutions that arise from the human element in GRC. We traverse the realms of social engineering, insider threats, and the nuanced interplay between technology and human behavior. We explore the paradox that technology, while offering both the sword and the shield, relies on individuals to choose which role it assumes.

"Beyond Checkboxes" is not simply a theoretical treatise on the subject; it is a pragmatic guide for practitioners, leaders, and security professionals who aspire to understand, empower, and ultimately fortify the human firewall within their organizations. It is a summons to transcend the routine of ticking boxes, and to embrace a deeper, more profound approach to GRC. One that recognizes and celebrates the irreplaceable role of humans in safeguarding our digital landscapes.

In the landscape of GRC, the traditional approach has been to rely heavily on technology, protocols, and frameworks. While these are vital components of a robust security and compliance strategy, they are not impervious to the ever-changing nature of digital threats. Cyber adversaries are adaptable, innovative, and often relentless in their pursuit of vulnerabilities. They have come to realize that one of the most fruitful avenues for exploiting these vulnerabilities lies within the very people who, knowingly or unknowingly, open doors and invite threats. In a world where technological advancements are swift and regulatory landscapes are complex, the human factor has emerged as both the catalyst for change and the most unpredictable variable in the equation.

This exploration of the human element in GRC is not an indictment of human beings or a criticism of the individuals who make up organizations. It is an acknowledgment of the complexities, challenges, and vulnerabilities inherent to the human condition. In a digital world where technology and data are ubiquitous, where our lives are intertwined with screens, networks, and information, the human element is the variable that can make or break the best-laid plans. It is the employees who can fall prey to a well-crafted phishing email, the executives who must balance the demand for innovation with the need for security, and the third-party vendors who must align with an organization's security protocols. It is, in essence, the collective actions, decisions, and behaviors of individuals within an organization that determine the efficacy of its GRC efforts.

As we journey deeper into the realm of the human element in GRC, we will traverse the territories of social engineering, where psychological manipulation and trust exploitation become the tools of malicious actors. We will delve into the complex challenges of insider threats, where the line between a trusted employee and a potential saboteur blurs. We will explore the intricate dance between the relentless evolution of technology and the behavior of individuals, revealing the duality of technology as both a source of vulnerabilities and a beacon of security.

The concepts we explore are not mere abstractions. They are the real-world challenges that organizations face every day. Incidents of data breaches, reputational damage, and compliance fines are not hypothetical scenarios but lived experiences for many. We will draw upon the lessons learned from such incidents, dissecting them to understand the underlying human factors that played a pivotal role.

However, this book is not just a journey into vulnerabilities and challenges. It is a guide to understanding, empowering, and fortifying the human element within your organization. It is a call to action to transform the traditional GRC approach into one that acknowledges the significance of the human factor. We provide pragmatic strategies for leaders, practitioners, and security professionals to develop a security-conscious workforce, nurture a culture of vigilance, and effectively align the human element with the technological and regulatory aspects of GRC.

Throughout this exploration, we will unveil the stories of organizations that have weathered storms and emerged stronger by embracing the human element as a strategic asset rather than a liability. These stories will serve as beacons of inspiration and practical guidance, illustrating how a focus on the human firewall can lead to a resilient and proactive GRC ecosystem.

In the chapters that follow, we will investigate the ways in which technology and human behavior intersect, examine the role of leadership in setting the tone for a security-aware organization, and explore emerging trends and future challenges that will shape the GRC landscape. We will delve into the legal and ethical obligations that come with data breaches and security incidents, emphasizing the importance of robust incident response and reporting mechanisms.

Join us on this transformative journey beyond the checkboxes, and into the heart of GRC. Here, we challenge preconceived notions, break free from the limitations of traditional GRC, and embark on a path that harnesses the true potential of the human element to safeguard our digital future. Welcome to a journey of discovery, empowerment, and transformation—a journey into "Beyond Checkboxes: The Human Element of GRC." It is our aspiration that this book will be your guide, mentor, and companion as you navigate the complexities of the GRC landscape, where the human element is the key to securing the future.

CHAPTER I

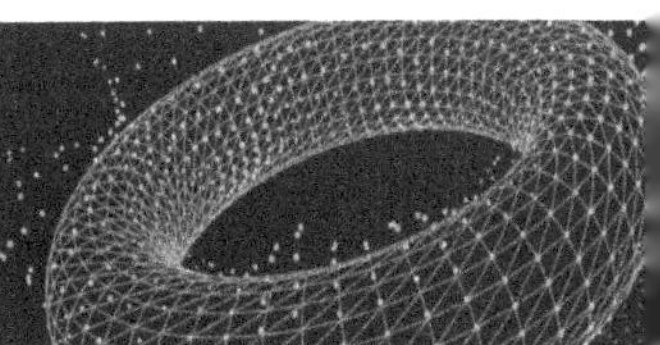

The Human Firewall: Strengthening the Weakest Link in Cybersecurity.

Understanding the Concept

In cybersecurity, the concept of the "human firewall" is a cornerstone in recognizing the importance of the human element in safeguarding an organization's digital assets. This subsection serves as the foundational component of the chapter, providing readers with a comprehensive understanding of what the human firewall entails.

Kevin Mitnick, late American computer security consultant, author, and convicted hacker once said ""Companies can spend millions of dollars on firewalls, encryption, and secure access devices, but it's a waste of money because none of the measures address the weakest link in the security chain: it's the person who uses, administers, operates, and is responsible for these systems." And no truer words have ever been said.

DEFINITION OF THE HUMAN FIREWALL

The concept of the human firewall represents a pivotal shift in the understanding of cybersecurity. It is a metaphorical construct that encapsulates the collective defense mechanisms, awareness, and actions of individuals within an organization to protect against cyber threats. In essence, the human firewall is the dynamic and ever-present line of defense that guards an organization's digital assets, information, and systems. It is not a tangible entity but a conceptual framework, one that underscores the irreplaceable role of people in fortifying the security perimeter.

At its core, the human firewall embodies the idea that security in the digital age is not solely about technological fortifications, encryption algorithms, or robust firewalls. While these technical aspects are crucial components of cybersecurity, they are only as effective as the people who manage, operate, and interact with them. The human element introduces a level of unpredictability, creativity, and adaptability that can both strengthen and challenge an organization's security measures. According to a study by IBM, 35% of data breaches can be attributed to human error. Another report indicated that human error resulted in a loss of about $3.33million dollars in 2020.

The term "human firewall" acknowledges that no matter how advanced the technology becomes, individuals within an organization remain the ultimate custodians of data and gatekeepers of access. They are the ones who, through their actions and decisions, determine whether an organization's defenses are resilient or vulnerable. Just as a physical firewall protects a building from external threats, the human firewall safeguards an organization from a wide array of digital threats, ranging from phishing attacks to insider threats.

The concept further recognizes that the human firewall is not a static or standalone entity. It evolves alongside the ever-changing landscape of cybersecurity threats. Cybercriminals continuously adapt their tactics and techniques, exploiting new vulnerabilities, and seeking novel ways to compromise security. Therefore, the human firewall must also adapt and evolve, staying vigilant, informed, and proactive in identifying and countering emerging threats.

In practical terms, the human firewall is nurtured through comprehensive training, a robust security-aware culture, well-defined security policies and procedures, and the continuous improvement of security measures. It involves empowering individuals at all levels of an organization to recognize and respond effectively to security threats, fostering a sense of responsibility for cybersecurity, and understanding the consequences of their actions on the organization's security posture.

Understanding the human firewall concept is the cornerstone of a human-centric approach to cybersecurity. It signifies a shift in perspective, from viewing individuals as potential liabilities to recognizing them as valuable assets in the ongoing battle against cyber threats. It is an acknowledgment that, in the digital age, the people factor is both the weakest link and the strongest defense, and the extent to which it is harnessed and fortified can make the critical difference in the cybersecurity resilience of any organization.

THE WEAKEST LINK IN CYBERSECURITY?

In the dynamic landscape of cybersecurity, the human element often emerges as the most unpredictable, and paradoxically, the most potent factor that can either bolster or compromise an organization's security defenses. This concept is rooted in the understanding that, despite the most advanced technological safeguards and rigorous compliance frameworks, it is the actions, behaviors, and decisions of individuals that can create vulnerabilities and serve as entry points for cyber threats. Let us delve into this concept with a GRC perspective:

Psychological Vulnerabilities: Human vulnerabilities in cybersecurity stem from a myriad of factors, many of which are deeply rooted in psychology. The human brain is susceptible to cognitive biases, such as confirmation bias, where individuals tend to favor information that confirms their preexisting beliefs, and authority bias, which leads people to follow authority figures without sound evaluation. Cybercriminals exploit these biases by crafting messages and scenarios that manipulate individuals into taking actions that compromise security.

Social Engineering Exploitation: Social engineering tactics, such as phishing, pretexting, baiting, and tailgating, rely on the human element's susceptibility to manipulation. Cybercriminals use these tactics to create a sense of urgency or trust, enticing individuals to divulge sensitive information, click on malicious links, or perform actions that lead to security breaches. The human factor is often the weakest link in the face of such psychologically crafted attacks.

Insider Threats: The human element extends beyond external threats to encompass insider threats. Employees and other individuals with access to an organization's systems can intentionally or unintentionally compromise security. Disgruntled employees, careless actions, or simply a lack of awareness can make the human element the weakest link, allowing insider threats to exploit their access.

Security Culture and Awareness: Recognizing that the human element plays a pivotal role in cybersecurity is an opportunity for organizations to cultivate a robust security culture. This involves not only technical training but also instilling a sense of responsibility and vigilance in employees at all levels. A security-aware culture can transform the human element from the weakest link into a proactive defense.

The Legal and Ethical Perspective: From a GRC standpoint, organizations must also consider the legal and ethical aspects. Compliance with data protection regulations, industry standards, and contractual obligations often hinges on the actions and decisions of individuals. Failure to uphold legal and ethical standards can lead to regulatory fines, legal repercussions, and damage to an organization's reputation.

Continuous Improvement and Adaptive Resilience: Recognizing the human element as the weakest link is not a criticism but an opportunity for continuous improvement and adaptive resilience. Organizations should continuously monitor and improve security awareness, educate employees, and implement behavioral analytics to detect anomalies. In doing so, the human element evolves from a liability to a proactive, adaptable, and resilient defense against cyber threats.

In subsequent chapters of this book, we will take even a closer look into these concepts individually and examine how they in turn contribute to the human factor being a loophole in cybersecurity.

We must hereby state that the concept of the human element being the weakest link in cybersecurity is a foundational principle in GRC. It acknowledges that the effectiveness of an organization's cybersecurity posture is intricately tied to the human behavior, decision-making, and security awareness of its personnel. It calls for a holistic approach to cybersecurity, where the human element is nurtured, educated, and empowered to be a proactive guardian of an organization's digital assets. Recognizing the potential of the human element to be a strong, rather than weak, link is a pivotal step toward comprehensive cyber risk management.

SIGNIFICANCE OF THE HUMAN FIREWALL

The significance of the human firewall lies in the role that employees, executives, and other stakeholders play in maintaining effective cybersecurity. Their actions, decisions, and awareness are pivotal in protecting an organization's digital assets, and this role is of paramount importance for several reasons:

First Line of Defense

Employees, from front-line staff to IT professionals, serve as the organization's initial response to potential threats. They are the eyes and ears that can detect and report anomalies, suspicious activities, and potential security breaches. Their role as the first line of defense is vital in preventing threats from escalating into serious incidents.

Protection of Sensitive Information

Employees have access to, and are custodians of, sensitive data, proprietary information, and critical systems. Their vigilance, adherence to security best practices, and responsible handling of data are fundamental in safeguarding these valuable assets. Negligence or security lapses can lead to data breaches and significant financial and reputational damage.

Mitigating Phishing and Social Engineering Threats

Phishing attacks and social engineering tactics rely on manipulating individuals through psychological and emotional triggers. Well-informed employees who are trained to recognize the signs of these attacks become a formidable defense against such tactics. Their ability to resist deception and make informed decisions is a critical aspect of the human firewall.

Executive Leadership and Tone Setting

Executives and leaders within an organization play a crucial role in setting the tone for cybersecurity. Their commitment to security initiatives, resource allocation for cybersecurity measures, and support for security awareness programs profoundly influence the organization's overall cybersecurity posture. When executives prioritize cybersecurity, it sends a clear message to the entire workforce that security is a core value.

Third-Party Vendor Risk Management

Many organizations rely on third-party vendors, suppliers, and partners to deliver products and services. These external entities can introduce vulnerabilities, and their security practices impact the organization. Employees involved in vendor relationships must assess third-party security measures, scrutinize contracts, and ensure that these partners adhere to cybersecurity best practices to mitigate risks introduced through these relationships.

Cultivating a Security-Aware Culture

The significance of the human firewall extends to fostering a security-aware culture across the organization. This culture encourages all stakeholders to view cybersecurity as a shared responsibility. When employees, executives, and third-party partners recognize their roles in protecting the organization's digital assets, a culture of vigilance and responsibility emerges. Security-aware individuals actively contribute to threat identification and mitigation.

Legal and Ethical Considerations

Employees and executives must be cognizant of the legal and ethical obligations surrounding cybersecurity. Compliance with data protection regulations, industry standards, and contractual obligations is not only a legal requirement but also a crucial element in maintaining a strong cybersecurity posture. Neglecting legal and ethical aspects can lead to regulatory fines, legal repercussions, and damage to an organization's reputation.

Continuous Learning and Adaptive Resilience

The human firewall is not static; it is a dynamic element that evolves alongside the ever-changing cybersecurity landscape. Employees and executives must engage in continuous learning, staying informed about the latest threats, and adapting security practices accordingly. The human firewall's ability to adapt and remain vigilant is a hallmark of its effectiveness.

The significance of the human firewall in cybersecurity cannot be overstated. It signifies a shift in perspective, recognizing that the people within an organization are not just potential liabilities but valuable assets to be nurtured, educated, and empowered as proactive guardians of digital assets. The human firewall concept underlines the potential of the human element to be a strong, rather than weak, link in the defense against cyber threats. It underscores the understanding that cybersecurity is not just a technical endeavor but deeply human, and its significance cannot be underestimated in the quest for comprehensive cyber risk management and resilient defense.

THE POTENTIAL CONSEQUENCES OF HUMAN ERRORS AND VULNERABILITIES IN CYBERSECURITY.

Human errors and vulnerabilities represent a profound and often underestimated aspect of the security equation. In this comprehensive analysis, we will explore the multifaceted consequences of human errors and vulnerabilities in cybersecurity, shedding light on the potential impacts they can have on organizations, their data, and their overall security posture.

UNDERSTANDING HUMAN ERRORS AND VULNERABILITIES

Before delving into the consequences, it's crucial to establish a clear understanding of what we mean by human errors and vulnerabilities in the context of cybersecurity.

Human Errors: These are non-malicious mistakes or oversights made by individuals within or outside an organization that can lead to security breaches. They encompass a wide range of actions, such as clicking on a phishing email, misconfiguring security settings, or inadvertently disclosing sensitive information. Human errors can stem from a lack of awareness, inadequate training, or simply a momentary lapse in judgment.

Human Vulnerabilities: These are the innate psychological and behavioral traits that make individuals susceptible to manipulation, deception, and social engineering tactics employed by cybercriminals. Vulnerabilities include cognitive biases like confirmation bias, which causes individuals to favor information that confirms their preexisting beliefs, and trust-based social dynamics that adversaries exploit to gain access to systems and data.

The tendency to ignore information and outright ignorance also falls within these contexts. Overlooking instructions as simple as updating the latest patch on an application is one of the easiest inlet most cyber criminals lookout for in their hunt for vulnerabilities in software or operating systems.

When software developers notice issues, they work on resolving them before they escalate and send patches to users long before data can be compromised. However, if due to the user's negligence they refuse to install the security update, it leaves room for them to fall prey and possibly other users too. A very popular example of a widespread data breach as a result of user's ignorance was Microsoft's WannaCry ransomware attack of 2017.

According to reports " it propagated by using EternalBlue, an exploit developed by the United States National Security Agency (NSA) for Windows systems. EternalBlue was stolen and leaked by a group called The Shadow Brokers a month prior to the attack. While Microsoft had released patches previously to close the exploit, much of WannaCry's spread was from organizations that had not applied these, or were using older Windows systems that were past their end-of-life. These patches were imperative to organizations' cyber security but many were not implemented due to ignorance of their importance. Some have claimed a need for 24/7 operation, aversion to risking having formerly working applications breaking because of patch changes, lack of personnel or time to install them, or other reasons. The attack was estimated to have affected more than 300,000 computers across 150 countries, with total damages ranging from hundreds of millions to billions of dollars."

The financial loss and damages could have been avoided entirely if only the users had taken the necessary steps in updating their security systems as expected.

Some other major ways human errors and vulnerabilities that can be exploited are Phishing and Social engineering.

THE ANATOMY OF A PHISHING ATTACK

In 'The Phishing Guide' by Gunter Ollman, Phishing is explained as the process of tricking or socially engineering an organization's customers into imparting their confidential information for nefarious use. Riding on the back of mass mailings such as spam, installing malware or using bots to automatically target victims, any online business may find phishers masquerading as them and targeting their customer base.

Phishing attacks have become increasingly sophisticated and often transparently mirror the site being targeted, allowing the attacker to observe everything while the victim is navigating the site, and transverse any additional security boundaries with the victim. Organizational size doesn't matter either; the quality of the personal information reaped from the attack has a value all in itself to the criminals.

Ollman also indicated that "Phishing attacks rely upon a mix of technical deceit and social engineering practices. In the majority of cases, the phisher must persuade the victim to intentionally perform a series of actions that will provide access to confidential information. Communication channels such as e-mail, web-pages, IRC and instant messaging services are popular. In all cases, the phisher must impersonate a trusted source for the victim to believe."

Social Engineering: The Manipulation of Trust

Phishers are virtuosos in the realm of social engineering, capitalizing on the innate human susceptibility to trust. They fabricate fake emails that emulate legitimate entities, often incorporating logos and branding elements to render them indistinguishable from genuine correspondences.

As proven by the July 15, 2020, Twitter breach, phishing attempts have expanded to include elements of social engineering. In one case, a 17-year-old hacker and his associates created a bogus website that resembled Twitter's internal VPN service, which was utilized by remote working workers.

Posing as helpdesk representatives, they phoned many Twitter workers and directed them to the bogus VPN website. They were able to take control of many high-profile user accounts, including those of Barack Obama, Elon Musk, Joe Biden, and Apple Inc.'s business account, using the information provided by the unknowing workers. The hackers then posted messages to their Twitter followers, offering to double the transaction amount in exchange for Bitcoin. The attackers received 12.86 BTC (about $117,000 at the time).

What Does A Typical Phishing Attack Look Like?

1. **The Bait: Crafted with Deception**

   A phishing attack embarks on a meticulous journey, commencing with the creation of an alluring bait, typically in the form of an email, message, or website. This bait is ingeniously designed to masquerade as something familiar and trustworthy, such as an email from a legitimate organization or a known individual, thus luring the victim into their deceptive web.

2. **The Hook: Coercion and Urgency**

Having set the bait, the attacker now resorts to psychological tactics to set the hook firmly into the victim.

* **Fear and Urgency: Precipitating Swift Action**

Phishers expertly play on human emotions, leveraging our fear of missing out or the urgency to act. Their choice of language often induces panic, with phrases like "Your account is compromised" or "Immediate action required," coercing individuals to click impulsively without due consideration.

* **Authority Impersonation: Posing as Trusted Figures**

To enhance credibility, attackers may impersonate authoritative figures, such as bank officials, colleagues, or government agencies. By usurping these figures' influence, they manipulate their victims, adding an extra layer of deception to their ruse.

TYPES OF PHISHING ATTACKS

SPEAR PHISHING: PERSONALIZED DECEPTION

While conventional phishing operations cast a broad net in hopes of ensnaring the unwary, spear phishing adopts a highly targeted approach. In this method, perpetrators invest substantial effort into researching their potential victims, gathering intelligence from social media and other sources to craft tailored messages that are nearly impossible to discern as fraudulent.

WHALING: GOING FOR THE BIG FISH

Whaling as a type of phishing attack is a focused effort of a cyber criminal aimed at targeting groups of high-level executives within a single organization, or executive positions common to multiple organizations. Whaling attacks are highly selective. Attackers carefully choose their targets, often focusing on individuals who have access to sensitive data, financial resources, or who can authorize significant transactions. Common targets include CEOs, CFOs, senior managers, and IT administrators.

The purpose is to steal their credentials - preferably by installing malware that grants the criminal a back-door functionality and key logging. The essence of this kind of focus on 'the big fish' of the organization is to achieve the highest likelihood of successfully breaching the security of the organization.

The Dark Art of Clone Phishing

Imagine a scenario where your email inbox pings with a message that appears to be from a familiar, trusted source—a colleague, a friend, or even your bank. The message seems genuine, and you decide to open it. Little do you know, you've just stepped into the world of clone phishing, a shadowy cyber tactic that can turn your online life upside down.

Clone phishing is not your run-of-the-mill cyber scam; it's an art form. Imagine an attacker meticulously crafting an email that mirrors a previous, legitimate message. The subject, the tone, and even the sender's address are all eerily accurate. You're hooked even before you know it.

Cyber criminals go to great lengths to make their replica emails look authentic. They'll replicate your friend's mannerisms, your colleague's jargon, or your bank's letterhead. They dive into your past communications, gleaning tidbits that make their clone emails virtually indistinguishable from the real deal.

The hook in clone phishing often comes in the form of a seemingly innocuous request, perhaps an attachment, a link, or the need to update your account information. They know how to pique your curiosity or stir your sense of responsibility. They're professionals at making you act on impulse.

Clone phishing is not limited to individuals. It threatens corporations, government agencies, and even infrastructure. Cyber criminals can masquerade as CEOs, HR departments, or IT support, aiming for sensitive corporate data, financial assets, or control of vital systems.

Voice Phishing (Vishing)

Voice phishing, or vishing, is a form of social engineering attack that involves the use of voice communication, typically phone calls, to deceive individuals into revealing sensitive information, such as personal identification numbers (PINs), credit card details, or login credentials. Vishing attacks aim to exploit human trust and gullibility by impersonating trusted entities or authority figures, often resulting in financial loss, data breaches, or identity theft.

The Basic Technique Employed

The techniques employed in vishing are similar to those one would come across in other forms of social engineering. They include;

* *Caller ID Spoofing*: Vishing attackers often manipulate caller ID information to make their calls appear legitimate. They might use software to display a number from a trusted organization, such as a bank or a government agency, further increasing their credibility.

* *Pretexting*: Attackers create fabricated scenarios or pretexts to engage with their targets, often pretending to be representatives from well-known companies or institutions. These fabricated scenarios can include threats of account closure, offers of financial incentives, or warnings about security breaches.

* *Impersonation*: Vishing attackers skillfully impersonate trusted entities, such as bank representatives, technical support personnel, or even law enforcement officers. They

use authoritative language and may reference personal information to seem more convincing.

SMS Phishing (Smishing)

SMS phishing, or smishing, is a social engineering attack that leverages short message service (SMS) text messages to deceive individuals into taking specific actions, such as clicking on malicious links, revealing personal information, or downloading malware onto their mobile devices. Smishing attacks have gained prominence due to the ubiquity of smartphones and the personal nature of SMS communication.

Understanding Smishing Techniques:

* *Deceptive Messages*: Smishing attacks begin with the victim receiving a text message that appears to come from a trusted source, such as a bank, a delivery service, a government agency, or even a friend. These messages may include urgent warnings, prize notifications, or fake security alerts to grab the recipient's attention.

* *Embedded Links*: The smishing message often includes links that, when clicked, direct the victim to a fraudulent website. These websites mimic legitimate ones, and victims may be prompted to enter sensitive information, such as login credentials or credit card details.

* *Call-to-Action*: The smishing message may include a strong call-to-action, urging the recipient to take immediate steps, such as clicking a link or responding with personal information.

Calendar Phishing

Calendar phishing, also known as calendar spam or calendar event phishing, exploits digital calendars and invitations to deceive individuals into taking malicious actions. It leverages calendar applications, like Google Calendar, Apple Calendar, or Microsoft

Outlook, and often manifests as unsolicited event invitations or spammy calendar entries.

CALENDAR PHISHING TECHNIQUES

* *Unsolicited Event Invitations*: Attackers send event invitations or calendar entries to the target's calendar application. These invitations often appear to be from reputable sources, and they can include enticing offers, fake surveys, or alarming alerts.

* *Social Engineering*: Calendar phishing relies on social engineering tactics, manipulating victims' curiosity, fear, or desire for rewards to encourage them to click on embedded links or provide sensitive information within the calendar event.

* *Deceptive Content*: Calendar phishing entries often include embedded links leading to malicious websites or forms requesting personal or financial information. These links may appear genuine at first glance.

PAGE HIJACKING: THE ELUSIVE THREAT

Page hijacking, also known as website page redirection, is a form of cyberattack in which malicious actors surreptitiously alter the content of a web page or redirect users to an unauthorized or malicious website. This unauthorized manipulation occurs without the knowledge or consent of the website owner or the visitor.

UNDERSTANDING PAGE HIJACKING TECHNIQUES:

* *Malicious Code Injection*: Attackers often exploit vulnerabilities in a website's code, commonly via cross-site scripting (XSS) or SQL injection, to inject malicious code. This code can redirect visitors to a different page, often designed to mimic a legitimate site, or to an attack vector.

* *DNS Manipulation*: Page hijacking can occur at the DNS level, where attackers tamper with Domain Name System settings to redirect users to malicious servers or sites.

* *Man-in-the-Middle Attacks (MitM)*: Sophisticated attackers may execute MitM attacks to intercept and modify web traffic, directing users to fake pages or intercepting sensitive data.

Arming the humans who have to mitigate these occurrences with the right knowledge becomes of utmost necessity. Learning to scrutinize even the smallest details and being cautious of unsolicited attachments and links can go a long way in preventing individuals and organizations from falling victim.

THE HUMAN FACTOR: VULNERABILITIES IN PLAY

In Hacking Humans: The Art of Exploiting Psychology in the Digital Age, by Daniel Cebo and Jason R. Sipper, they highlighted how hacking has gone beyond attack on systems and progressed to the humans who use the systems, "In our increasingly interconnected world, where technology permeates every aspect of our lives, the concept of hacking has expanded beyond traditional computer systems. Now, we find ourselves confronting the unsettling notion of hacking humans, the manipulation and exploitation of individuals through psychological, social, and technological means." This goes to show that as much as we need to protect systems from threats, vulnerabilities in humans also need to be understood and shielded from exploitation as well. Some of these vulnerabilities appear in the form of:

1. Cognitive Biases: The Achilles' Heel

Confirmation Bias

Confirmation bias compels individuals to interpret information in a manner that validates their pre-existing beliefs. Phishers cunningly exploit this bias by structuring their emails in a way that aligns with what the victim anticipates, thereby diminishing skepticism.

Reciprocity

Phishers manipulate the principle of reciprocity, a potent psychological trigger, by offering a small token, such as a "free" e-book or a discount. This gesture creates a sense of obligation in recipients, nudging them towards clicking links or divulging sensitive information.

Curiosity

The intrinsic human curiosity becomes a vulnerability that phishers deftly exploit. Subject lines that appeal to curiosity, such as "See this shocking video" or "Unbelievable discount," engage recipients' interest, enticing them to take the bait.

2. Trust in Technology

False Sense of Security

Phishing victims often harbor a misguided sense of security, trusting their antivirus software or email filters to shield them from harm. This unwarranted self-assurance can breed complacency, leading individuals to be less cautious about the emails they open.

Trust in Visual Cues

Phishers routinely leverage official logos, SSL certificates, and familiar web designs to lend authenticity to their emails and websites. Recipients unwittingly place their trust in these visual cues, using them to validate the legitimacy of the correspondence.

Now, let's explore the potential consequences of these human errors and vulnerabilities in cybersecurity:

1. **Data Breaches and Loss of Confidential Information**

   Human errors are often at the core of data breaches. Inadvertently sharing login credentials, mishandling sensitive documents, or falling victim to phishing attacks can result in unauthorized access to an organization's systems. When confidential information falls into the wrong hands, the consequences can be severe. This may include the exposure of customer data, intellectual property theft, and breaches of legal and regulatory compliance, potentially leading to financial and reputational damage.

2. **Financial Loss and Legal Consequences**

   Data breaches and cyber incidents resulting from human errors can lead to significant financial losses. Organizations may face not only the costs associated with breach remediation but also regulatory fines and legal actions. Failure to protect customer data can result in non-compliance with data protection laws, such as the General Data Protection Regulation (GDPR) or the Health Insurance Portability and Accountability Act (HIPAA), leading to substantial penalties.

3. **Reputational Damage**

   Reputation is a valuable asset for any organization. A data breach or security incident caused by human errors can tarnish an organization's reputation, eroding trust among customers, partners, and stakeholders. Negative publicity and the perception that the organization cannot adequately protect sensitive information can have long-lasting consequences.

4. Insider Threats and Sabotage

While the focus is often on external threats, the human element can also pose significant risks. Insiders, whether acting with malicious intent or unintentionally, can exploit their knowledge and access to compromise security. They may engage in corporate espionage, intellectual property theft, or even sabotage an organization's operations.

5. Operational Disruption

Human vulnerabilities, such as susceptibility to social engineering tactics, can lead to operational disruption. Cybercriminals may exploit trust-based relationships or manipulate individuals into making unauthorized changes to systems or transferring funds. This can disrupt normal business operations, causing downtime and financial losses.

6. Compliance Violations

Adherence to regulatory requirements is essential in various industries, such as finance, healthcare, and e-commerce. Human errors and vulnerabilities can lead to compliance violations, which, in turn, can result in regulatory fines and legal repercussions. Ensuring that employees handle sensitive data and systems in compliance with industry standards and legal requirements is an ongoing challenge.

7. Intellectual Property Theft

Organizations invest heavily in research and development to create intellectual property that provides a competitive edge. Human errors can expose intellectual property to theft or compromise. In industries where innovation is a key differentiator, the loss of intellectual property can erode an organization's competitive advantage.

8. **Trust Erosion**

Erosion of trust extends beyond reputational damage. It can affect relationships with customers, partners, and employees. When stakeholders lose trust in an organization's ability to protect their information, they may seek alternatives, leading to customer churn and partner disengagement.

9. **Increased Cybersecurity Costs**

The aftermath of human errors and vulnerabilities often necessitates investments in cybersecurity enhancements, incident response, and employee training. These costs can strain an organization's budget and resources.

10. **Impact on Business Continuity**

Operational disruptions resulting from security incidents can affect an organization's ability to maintain business continuity. This can lead to lost revenue, missed opportunities, and difficulties in recovering from the incident.

11. **Complex Incident Response**

Incident response becomes more complex when human errors or vulnerabilities are involved. Investigating incidents, determining the extent of the breach, and mitigating the damage can be challenging, often requiring a multifaceted approach to address both technical and human factors.

12. **Psychological Impact on Employees**

Employees who fall victim to phishing attacks or make errors that lead to security incidents may experience a sense of guilt, stress, or anxiety. This psychological impact can affect their well-being and productivity.

13. Impact on Brand Equity

The consequences of human errors and vulnerabilities can reverberate through the brand equity of an organization. Brands that are associated with frequent data breaches or security incidents may struggle to regain the trust of their target audience.

STRENGTHENING THE HUMAN FIREWALL

Considering the level of loss that comes with data breaches in most cases, it goes without saying that the human factor needs to be supported to function optimally.

The outline below details an all-encompassing process for strengthening the human firewall within any organization as a vital component in cybersecurity:

STEP 1: DEFINE THE SCOPE AND OBJECTIVES

SCOPE DEFINITION

Begin by identifying the specific areas, roles, and processes within the organization that need reinforcement to build a robust human firewall. Here is how to define scope and objectives when embarking on this task:

Understand the Organization: Gain a thorough understanding of your organization's structure, size, culture, and industry. This context is important for determining the extent of your human firewall strengthening efforts.

Identify Assets and Data: Clearly define the sensitive assets, data, and information that need protection. Identify where this data resides, how it's accessed, and the potential vulnerabilities associated with it.

Define the Human Element: Recognize that the human element encompasses employees, contractors, and other stakeholders. Determine which roles, teams, or departments are most essential to the organization's cybersecurity.

Map Human Touchpoints: Identify the touchpoints where human actions intersect with cybersecurity, such as email communication, access to high-priority systems, or handling of sensitive data. These are the areas where the human firewall will be strengthened.

Consider External Factors: Take into account external factors, such as the regulatory environment, industry standards, and emerging threats. These factors can influence the scope of your efforts.

Identify Vulnerabilities: Conduct a risk assessment to identify vulnerabilities related to human factors. This can include social engineering, password management, training gaps, and more.

Incorporate Compliance Requirements: Ensure that your scope is aligned with legal and regulatory compliance requirements, such as GDPR, HIPAA, or industry-specific standards.

OBJECTIVES SETTING

Clearly define the objectives you want to achieve, such as reducing the risk of social engineering attacks, improving incident reporting, or enhancing overall security awareness. The process of clearly defining your objectives involves:

SMART Objectives: Ensure that your objectives are Specific, Measurable, Achievable, Relevant, and Time-bound (SMART) to make them clear, quantifiable, and actionable.

* *Specific*: Objectives should clearly state what needs to be achieved. For example, "Reduce the rate of successful phishing attacks by 50% within one year."

* *Measurable*: Include specific metrics or KPIs to measure progress. For example, "Increase the percentage of employees who complete annual cybersecurity training from 60% to 90% within six months."

* *Achievable*: Objectives should be realistic and attainable within the available resources, such as budget, time, and personnel.

* *Relevant*: Ensure that the objectives align with the organization's broader cybersecurity goals and mission. They should directly contribute to strengthening the human firewall.

* *Time-bound*: Set clear timeframes for achieving the objectives. This adds a sense of urgency and helps with monitoring and accountability.

* *Prioritize Objectives:* If you have multiple objectives, prioritize them based on their significance and impact on your organization's security. For instance, prioritize objectives related to vital assets and high-risk areas.

* *Consult Stakeholders:* Involve key stakeholders, including IT, HR, legal, and employees, in the objective-setting process. Their input and buy-in are crucial for success.

* *Training and Awareness Objectives:* Include specific objectives related to employee training, awareness campaigns, and incident response readiness.

* *Monitoring and Feedback:* Establish a process for continuous monitoring, measurement, and feedback to assess progress and adapt objectives as needed.

STEP 2: ASSESS CURRENT STATE

GAP ANALYSIS

Gap analysis is a valuable process in strengthening the human firewall, as it helps organizations identify the disparities between their current state of cybersecurity and their desired, more secure state. This analysis guides the development of strategies and actions to bridge those gaps effectively. It also involves documenting all aspects of the gap analysis, including findings, action plans, progress reports, and outcomes. This documentation is essential for compliance, audit, and reporting purposes.

By conducting a comprehensive gap analysis and systematically addressing the identified weaknesses in your human firewall, you can make substantial improvements to your organization's cybersecurity posture and mitigate risks associated with human factors.

RISK ASSESSMENT

This is another crucial step in identifying and mitigating vulnerabilities and threats associated with the human element in any organization's cybersecurity. It aids in systematically identifying, prioritizing and addressing issues identified before they can be taken advantage of by guiding the organization's focus in the strengthening process.

STEP 3: POLICY AND PROCEDURE DEVELOPMENT

SECURITY POLICIES

Developing or updating security policies that define acceptable behaviors and security practices within the organization is a crucial element that must not be overlooked. The organization must ensure that policies are clear, accessible, and aligned with industry standards and regulations.

The aim should be to develop cybersecurity policies that cover various areas such as data protection, access controls, password management, acceptable use, social engineering awareness, and incident response.

A good place to start is to clearly define the scope and objectives of each policy. What is the policy meant to achieve, and which areas does it cover?

* *Responsibilities*: Outline the roles and responsibilities of employees, IT, management, and any other relevant stakeholders in implementing the policy.

* *Compliance Requirements*: Ensure that policies align with relevant laws, regulations, and industry standards. If necessary, involve legal experts to review the policies for compliance.

* *Enforcement and Consequences:* Clearly state the consequences of policy violations, including disciplinary actions. Employees should understand the importance of compliance.

PROCEDURES

Define specific procedures and guidelines for employees to follow, covering topics like password management, incident reporting, and safe data handling. This can be loosely broken down into;

* *Incident Reporting Procedure:* How should employees report security incidents or breaches? Who should they contact, and what information should they provide?

* *Training and Awareness Procedure:* Outline the process for providing cybersecurity training to employees, including the frequency and content.

* *Access Control Procedure:* Specify how access to sensitive data or systems is granted, monitored, and revoked.

* *Password Management Procedure:* Explain the requirements for creating and managing secure passwords.

* *Social Engineering Awareness Procedure*: Describe how employees should recognize and respond to social engineering attempts.

STEP 4: EMPLOYEE TRAINING AND AWARENESS

SECURITY AWARENESS PROGRAMME

Employee training and awareness can never be overemphasized. It is a major determinant in how staff recognize and respond to cybersecurity threats and how effectively they do so. They need to be equipped for the task and be reminded often these measures are provided.

Implement comprehensive security awareness programs that educate employees on security best practices, social engineering threats, and the importance of the human firewall.

A sample process to follow is;

1. **Needs Assessment**

    Begin with a thorough assessment of your organization's specific needs. This should take into account the organization's size, industry, current level of cybersecurity awareness, and potential risks related to the human element.

2. **Define Training Objectives:**

    Clearly define the objectives of the training program. What do you want employees to learn and achieve through the training? Objectives should be SMART (Specific, Measurable, Achievable, Relevant, and Time-bound).

3. **Identify Target Audiences:**

    Identify the specific employee groups or roles that require different levels or types of training. For example, IT staff may need different training than non-technical employees.

4. **Develop Training Content:**

   Develop comprehensive training materials that cover various cybersecurity topics, including:

   * *Cybersecurity Basics*: **Introduce fundamental concepts of cybersecurity, including common threats and best practices.**

   * *Social Engineering Awareness*: **Educate employees about different forms of social engineering, such as phishing, pretexting, and tailgating.**

   * *Password Security:* **Provide guidelines for creating strong passwords and secure password management.**

   * *Data Protection:* **Explain the importance of safeguarding sensitive information and data handling best practices.**

   * *Incident Response:* **Outline the steps employees should take if they suspect a security incident or breach.**

   * *Compliance Requirements:* **Address specific legal and regulatory requirements that apply to your organization.**

5. **Training Methods**

   Choose appropriate training methods based on your organization's culture and the needs of your employees. Common methods include:

   * *eLearning Modules:* **Interactive online courses that employees can complete at their own pace.**

   * *In-Person Workshops:* **On-site or virtual workshops led by cybersecurity experts.**

* *Simulated Phishing Exercises:* **Conduct regular simulated phishing campaigns to test and reinforce employee awareness.**

* *Security Awareness Videos:* **Short, engaging videos that address specific cybersecurity topics.**

6. **Training Schedule**

   Develop a training schedule that outlines when and how often training sessions will occur. Consider providing initial training for new employees and regular refresher courses for all staff.

7. **Communication Plan**

   Communicate the training schedule, objectives, and expectations to employees. Ensure that they are aware of the importance of cybersecurity training and their role in the organization's security.

8. **Training Delivery:**

   Deliver training sessions using the chosen methods. Be sure to accommodate different learning styles, and consider providing a variety of resources to cater to individual preferences.

9. **Assessment and Evaluation:**

   After training sessions, assess employees' understanding and awareness of cybersecurity topics. Use quizzes, tests, or surveys to evaluate their knowledge.

10. **Feedback and Continuous Improvement:**

    Encourage employees to provide feedback on the training program. Use their input to improve the quality and relevance of the content and delivery methods.

11. Reinforcement and Simulations:

Regularly conduct simulated phishing exercises to test employees' ability to recognize and respond to phishing attempts. Use these exercises as learning opportunities.

12. Awareness Campaigns:

Develop ongoing cybersecurity awareness campaigns to reinforce training messages. Use posters, newsletters, and email reminders to keep cybersecurity top of mind.

13. Incident Reporting Guidance:

Train employees on how to recognize and report security incidents. Ensure they know whom to contact and what information to provide in case of a potential breach.

14. Monitoring and Reporting:

Continuously monitor the effectiveness of the training and awareness program. Use key performance indicators (KPIs) to track improvements and areas that may need additional attention.

15. Compliance and Record-Keeping:

Maintain documentation of training and awareness activities, including attendance records, quiz scores, and feedback. This documentation is essential for compliance and auditing purposes.

16. Periodic Review and Updates:

Regularly review and update training materials and methods to keep the program relevant and aligned with emerging threats and technologies.

17. **Phishing Simulations:**

    Conduct regular phishing simulations to test employees' ability to recognize and respond to phishing attempts. Use these exercises to reinforce training and measure improvement.

Step 5: Access Control and User Authentication

ACCESS CONTROL POLICIES

As the cybersecurity terrain becomes more difficult to navigate, organizations are always encouraged to implement robust access control policies to ensure that employees only have access to the resources necessary for their roles.

These measures help ensure that only authorized individuals have access to sensitive data and systems thereby reducing the incidence of a breach.

Strongdm, a tech company that helps organizations manage and audit access to their databases, servers, clusters and web applications identify 3 common types of access control which are;

1. *Discretionary Access Control (DAC):* Access permissions are granted based on the regulations previously established by the administrators. In this access control approach, each resource has an owner or administrator who selects who has access and at what level.

2. *Role-based Access Control (RBAC):* rather than considering a single user account inside a corporation, system administrators utilize the RBAC (or non-discretionary) access control paradigm to provide access based on organizational responsibilities. Only those with positions that need the specific work have access to the resource.

3. *Attribute-based Access Control(ABAC):* compared to the role-defined access control method of RBAC, ABAC uses a broader strategy that applies a myriad of attributes to both the users and resources. It gives admins the flexibility to make decisions according to context and evolving level of risks.

To carry out an access control and user authentication process for an organization successfully, the process below details a simple approach to take;

1. **Assess Access Needs:**

   Begin by conducting an assessment to understand the specific access requirements of employees and third parties. Determine who needs access to what resources and why.

2. **Identify Sensitive Resources:**

   Identify the sensitive data, systems, applications, and areas of your organization that require robust access control. These may include customer data, financial systems, proprietary information, and important infrastructure.

3. **Determine Access Levels:**

   Define different access levels or roles within your organization. For example, you may have different access levels for employees, contractors, and administrators, each with varying permissions.

4. **Compliance and Regulatory Considerations:**

   Ensure that access control measures align with relevant compliance requirements and regulations, such as GDPR, HIPAA, or industry-specific standards.

5. **Access Control Policies:**

   Develop comprehensive access control policies that outline the principles, procedures, and guidelines for access management. These policies should cover areas like user account creation, provisioning, deprovisioning, and permissions.

6. **User Authentication Methods:**

Determine the authentication methods that will be used to verify the identity of users before granting access. Common methods include passwords, multi-factor authentication (MFA), biometrics, and smart cards.

7. **Password Policies:**

Establish password policies that guide employees on creating strong, unique passwords and implementing secure password management practices. Password policies should specify length, complexity, expiration, and change requirements.

8. **Role-Based Access Control (RBAC):**

Implement role-based access control, where access permissions are based on an individual's role within the organization. Ensure that employees are granted the minimum level of access necessary to perform their job functions.

9. **User Account Management:**

Develop procedures for creating, modifying, and disabling user accounts. Specify the workflow for user onboarding, changes in roles, and offboarding.

10. **Account Review and Recertification:**

Regularly review user accounts and permissions to ensure they are up-to-date and necessary. Implement a recertification process to verify and revalidate access rights.

11. **Access Requests and Approvals:**

Create a system for users to request access and for administrators to approve or deny those requests. This process should be well-documented and include proper authorization.

Multi-Factor Authentication (MFA): Encourage the use of MFA to add an additional layer of security to account access, reducing the risk of unauthorized access.

STEP 6: INCIDENT RESPONSE AND REPORTING

INCIDENT RESPONSE PLAN

The main goal here is to effectively manage incidents to minimize damage to systems, data, reduce recovery time and cost and control damage to brand reputation.

Organizations therefore must develop and maintain a well-defined incident response plan that outlines the steps to take in case of a security incident or breach involving the human firewall.

An incident response plan helps an organization in three major ways:

1. To prepare for known and unknown circumstances.

2. To immediately identify attempts or successful compromise in their security setup.

3. To establish best practices to block intrusions before they cause damage.

A standard incident response and reporting plan that may be implemented by an organization includes the following;

1. **Preparing for Incidents:**

   Begin by having a comprehensive incident response plan (IRP) in place. Ensure it includes specific procedures for handling incidents that involve human factors, such as social engineering attacks or insider threats.

2. **Incident Identification:**

   Train employees to recognize signs of security incidents, including unusual system behavior, phishing attempts, unauthorized access, or data breaches.

3. **Incident Reporting:**

   Establish clear and easy-to-follow reporting channels for employees to report potential security incidents. This can include email, a dedicated hotline, or an incident reporting portal. Ensure that reporting is anonymous and free from retaliation.

4. **Incident Triage:**

   Upon receiving an incident report, the incident response team assesses the incident's severity and impact. This assessment helps in prioritizing responses.

5. **Response Team Activation:**

   Activate the incident response team, which should include IT professionals, legal experts, communication specialists, and relevant stakeholders. Ensure that team members are aware of their roles and responsibilities.

6. **Containment and Mitigation:**

   Take immediate actions to contain the incident and mitigate the damage. This may involve isolating affected systems, revoking unauthorized access, or implementing security patches.

7. **Evidence Preservation:**

    In cases involving insider threats or other potential human-related incidents, preserve evidence and maintain chain of custody to support investigations.

8. **Investigation:**

    Conduct a thorough investigation to determine the cause, source, and extent of the incident. Involve forensics experts if necessary to collect and analyze evidence.

9. **Legal and Compliance Considerations:**

    Ensure that all actions taken during the incident response process comply with legal and regulatory requirements, including data breach notification laws.

10. **Documentation:**

    Maintain detailed records of the incident, including actions taken, findings, and communication logs. These records are valuable for post-incident analysis, audits, and compliance reporting.

11. **Post-Incident Review:**

    Conduct a post-incident review to evaluate the effectiveness of the response. Identify areas for improvement in policies, procedures, and technology solutions.

12. **Technology and Process Enhancements:**

    Use incident response experiences to enhance access controls, authentication methods, and security policies, reducing the risk of future incidents.

Step 7: Continuous Monitoring and Improvement

Having and executing a plan is merely just the beginning in the process of fortifying your human firewalls, there must also be continuous monitoring and improvement for the process to rain viable at all times. A common yardstick many organizations use in setting up parameters for this process include:

1. **Establishing Key Performance Indicators (KPIs):**

    Define KPIs that align with your organization's cybersecurity objectives. These metrics will serve as benchmarks for measuring the effectiveness of your human firewall and training programs.

2. **Monitoring Employee Compliance:**

    Regularly assess employee compliance with security policies and procedures. Use surveys, quizzes, or simulated phishing exercises to evaluate their adherence to best practices.

3. **Incident Response Data Analysis:**

    Analyze data from previous security incidents, including incident reports and response activities. Identify recurring patterns or trends related to human-related vulnerabilities and threats.

4. **Security Awareness and Training Metrics:**

    Track training completion rates, quiz scores, and employee feedback from cybersecurity training and awareness programs. Use this data to assess the effectiveness of your training efforts.

5. **Phishing Simulation Results:**

    Review the results of simulated phishing exercises, including click rates, response times, and user feedback. Identify areas where employees are most susceptible to social engineering attacks.

6. Employee Feedback and Suggestions:

Encourage employees to provide feedback on security practices and report potential vulnerabilities. Regularly gather their input to understand their perspective and concerns.

7. Incident Reporting Analysis:

Examine incident reports and their resolutions. Assess whether incident reporting channels are effective and whether the response process has room for improvement.

8. Root Cause Analysis:

Conduct root cause analyses of security incidents to identify the underlying reasons for their occurrence. Determine whether they are due to human errors, system weaknesses, or other factors.

9. Periodic Security Assessments:

Schedule periodic security assessments and audits, including vulnerability assessments, penetration testing, and access control reviews. These assessments can help uncover vulnerabilities and weaknesses in your security measures.

10. Industry Benchmarking:

Compare your organization's security posture with industry benchmarks and best practices. Identify areas where you may be lagging behind or excelling.

By following this process, you can ensure that your organization's human firewall remains strong and adaptable to emerging threats. Continuous monitoring and improvement are key to staying proactive and reducing risks associated with human factors in cybersecurity.

STEP 8: COMPLIANCE AND LEGAL CONSIDERATIONS

Adhering to relevant laws and regulations is essential to protect sensitive data, maintain trust, and avoid legal consequences. A things to take into considerations in this aspect are:

1. **Data Protection Regulations:**
   * *Compliance*: Ensure compliance with data protection regulations, such as the European Union's General Data Protection Regulation (GDPR) or the California Consumer Privacy Act (CCPA). These regulations impose strict requirements for the protection of personal and sensitive data.

   * *Legal Considerations*: Failure to comply with these regulations can lead to severe fines and legal consequences. Strengthening the human firewall involves educating employees on data protection requirements and ensuring that they follow best practices for data handling.

2. **Industry-Specific Regulations:**
   * *Compliance*: Certain industries have specific regulations that pertain to the safeguarding of information, like the Health Insurance Portability and Accountability Act (HIPAA) for healthcare organizations or the Payment Card Industry Data Security Standard (PCI DSS) for businesses that handle payment card information.

   * *Legal Considerations*: Non-compliance with industry-specific regulations can result in regulatory fines, lawsuits, and damage to an organization's reputation. Ensuring employees understand and follow these regulations is a key aspect of the human firewall.

3. **Security Incident Reporting Laws:**

   * *Compliance*: Many regions and countries have laws that require organizations to report security incidents promptly. Compliance with these laws may necessitate specific incident response procedures and timelines.

   * *Legal Considerations*: Failure to report security incidents in a timely manner can lead to regulatory penalties and, in some cases, legal actions. Employees should be aware of the legal obligations and their role in incident reporting.

4. **Employee Privacy Laws:**

   * *Compliance*: In some jurisdictions, there are laws protecting employee privacy rights, which may limit the extent to which employers can monitor and access employee data. Compliance is necessary to respect these legal boundaries.

   * *Legal Considerations*: Violating employee privacy laws can result in lawsuits and legal liabilities. Organizations must strike a balance between cybersecurity monitoring and respecting employee privacy rights.

5. **Employment Laws:**

   * *Compliance*: Employment laws, including labor regulations, vary by region and may affect the implementation of security policies, employee monitoring, and disciplinary actions related to cybersecurity.

   * *Legal Considerations*: Failing to comply with employment laws can result in legal disputes and challenges from employees. Organizations must tailor their human firewall strategies within the confines of these laws.

6. **Cybersecurity Liability Laws:**

   * *Compliance*: Some jurisdictions have laws outlining the liability of organizations for cybersecurity breaches and data loss. Complying with these laws may require specific preventive measures and incident response plans.

   * *Legal Considerations*: Neglecting cybersecurity liability laws can lead to legal actions by affected parties or regulatory bodies. Employee training is essential to reduce the likelihood of breaches that could lead to legal consequences.

7. **Legal Agreements and Contracts:**

   * *Compliance*: Ensure that your organization's legal agreements and contracts, including service-level agreements (SLAs) and third-party agreements, reflect your cybersecurity requirements and the responsibilities of all parties involved.

   * *Legal Considerations*: Breach of contractual agreements may lead to legal disputes and financial liabilities. Employees should understand the implications of these agreements and their role in compliance.

8. **Intellectual Property Protection:**

   * *Compliance*: Protect your organization's intellectual property by complying with patent, copyright, and trademark laws. Educate employees about the importance of safeguarding proprietary information.

   * *Legal Considerations*: Violations of intellectual property laws can result in lawsuits and damage to the organization's intellectual assets. Ensuring that employees recognize the value of intellectual property is a key part of the human firewall.

9. **Compliance Documentation:**

* *Compliance*: Maintain thorough documentation of your organization's compliance efforts, including training records, incident response logs, and any other relevant records. This documentation is essential for audits and legal defense.

* *Legal Considerations*: By addressing these compliance and legal considerations, your organization can effectively strengthen your staff while minimizing legal risks and ensuring that employees are aware of their responsibilities and legal obligations.

STEP 9: LEADERSHIP, COMMUNICATION AND CULTURE

Brian Chesky, the Co-founder and CEO, Airbnb once said "Why is culture so important to a business? Here is a simple way to frame it. The stronger the culture, the less corporate process a company needs. When the culture is strong, you can trust everyone to do the right thing." Exemplary leadership and a strong culture of cybersecurity, supported by effective communication, fosters a security-conscious environment and helps employees become an active line of defense against cyber threat. When the culture is in place, getting employees to do their part is less tasking. To achieve this, an organization must create an enabling environment through the process of:

* *Leadership Buy-In:* Senior leadership sets the tone for a cybersecurity culture. When executives prioritize security and lead by example, it reinforces the importance of security throughout the organization.

* *Inclusivity:* Cultivate an inclusive culture where all employees feel responsible for cybersecurity. This includes not only IT personnel but individuals from all departments.

* *Varied Channels:* Utilize a variety of communication channels, such as emails, newsletters, intranet portals, and in-person meetings, to disseminate information about cybersecurity. Reach employees through channels they are most comfortable with.

* *Multi-Directional Communication:* Encourage multi-directional communication, allowing employees to ask questions, seek clarifications, and report concerns. An open communication culture promotes engagement and trust.

* *Accountability:* Promote a culture of accountability, where employees understand that they play a significant role in maintaining security. Everyone should know that their actions or inactions can impact the organization's cybersecurity posture.

* *Rewards and Recognition:* Recognize and reward employees for their contributions to security, such as reporting incidents, adhering to policies, or participating in awareness initiatives. Positive reinforcement helps build a security-focused culture.

Building the people involved in your defense might be a challenging task but holds infinite rewards. In the long run, your employees are not only aware of potential threats to the security of your system but are also motivated to be vigilant and proactive in guarding against risks.

STEP 10: ONGOING GOVERNANCE AND OVERSIGHT

In order to achieve all that we have discussed so far, organizations need a structured approach to managing, maintaining and continuously improving cybersecurity measures related to the human element.

Governance and oversight creates a continuous feedback loop that incorporates insights from audits, incidents and monitoring to enhance security measures and practices. A well-governed process allows organizations to adapt to emerging cybersecurity threats and trends by adjusting policies, procedures and training methods as required.

In effect, ongoing governance and oversight are essential for maintaining the strength of the human firewall by ensuring policy adherence, mitigating risks, complying with regulations, sustaining employee training and awareness, optimizing access control and authentication, enhancing incident response and reporting, fostering a culture of cybersecurity, aligning technology and processes, maintaining documentation and reporting, and enabling continuous improvement. These processes help organizations respond effectively to the dynamic nature of cybersecurity threats and vulnerabilities.

REAL-LIFE CASE STUDIES OF SECURITY BREACHES DUE TO HUMAN ERROR

Despite the dedicated efforts organizations put into increasing their security investment over the past decade, many are still plagued by data breaches. In fact, we are learning that of all the data breaches that have occurred in recent years, human error accounts for 95% of such occurrences either directly or indirectly.

It is imperative there that we take a look at some that have happened in recent times, what led to them, their impact and lessons learned.

Target Data Breach (2013):

* *Human Error:* A contractor's credentials were stolen through a phishing email. The contractor had access to Target's network and point-of-sale (POS) systems.

* *Impact*: Hackers exploited the compromised credentials to install malware on Target's POS systems, leading to the theft of credit card and personal information from over 40 million customers.

* *Lessons Learned:* This breach underscored the importance of employee training in recognizing phishing emails and the need to limit and monitor third-party access to sensitive systems.

Equifax Data Breach (2017):

* *Human Error:* Equifax failed to apply a patch to a known vulnerability in their Apache Struts software.

* *Impact:* The breach exposed the personal information of 143 million consumers. It was one of the largest data breaches in history.

* Lessons Learned: The breach highlighted the key role of patch management and timely application of security updates.

WannaCry Ransomware Attack (2017):

* *Human Error:* Many organizations were affected by the WannaCry ransomware because they failed to apply a very important Microsoft Windows patch.

* *Impact:* The ransomware infected hundreds of thousands of computers worldwide, causing widespread disruption, data loss, and financial losses.

* *Lessons Learned:* The incident emphasized the importance of keeping software up-to-date to prevent known vulnerabilities from being exploited.

Capital One Data Breach (2019):

* *Human Error:* A former employee exploited a misconfigured firewall to gain unauthorized access to Capital One's systems.

* *Impact:* The breach exposed the personal information of over 100 million customers. It included credit card applications, Social Security numbers, and bank account numbers.

* *Lessons Learned:* Organizations must ensure proper configuration and access controls for their systems, as well as monitor and audit employee access.

Twitter Bitcoin Scam (2020):

* *Human Error:* Hackers gained access to Twitter's internal tools by social engineering Twitter employees.

* *Impact:* The attackers used these tools to hijack high-profile accounts and post a Bitcoin scam, resulting in financial losses for individuals who fell for the scam.

* *Lessons Learned:* The incident highlighted the need for robust social engineering awareness training for employees who have access to vital tools and accounts.

SolarWinds Supply Chain Attack (2020):

* *Human Error:* Hackers compromised SolarWinds' software update mechanism, resulting in the distribution of malicious updates to numerous customers.

* *Impact:* Multiple government agencies and businesses were affected. Sensitive data and intellectual property were compromised.

* *Lessons Learned:* The breach demonstrated the importance of supply chain security, third-party risk management, and the need to scrutinize software updates.

In essence, individuals and organizations must understand that the role of humans in preventing such occurrences is an important one that needs to be constantly monitored, elevated and fortified as often as possible.

ASSESSMENT FRAMEWORKS: EXPLORING THE EFFECTIVENESS OF EFFORTS TO STRENGTHEN THE HUMAN FIREWALL

An assessment framework is the process of evaluating the effectiveness of all efforts channeled towards improving the cybersecurity posture of an organization and identifying areas for improvement.

There are several frameworks and metrics that can help organizations assess the impact of their initiatives in this regard. Some of them include:

NIST Cybersecurity Framework:

* *Framework Overview:* The National Institute of Standards and Technology (NIST) Cybersecurity Framework is a widely adopted framework for managing and reducing cybersecurity risk. It includes functions like Identify, Protect, Detect, Respond, and Recover.

* *Metrics:* Organizations can use a combination of metrics such as the number of security incidents, incident response times, training completion rates, and the frequency of phishing simulations to assess the effectiveness of their human firewall efforts.

CIS Controls:

* *Framework Overview:* The Center for Internet Security (CIS) Controls provides a prioritized set of actions to improve an organization's cybersecurity posture. The controls include guidelines related to asset management, access control, and employee training.

* *Metrics:* Metrics for assessing the human firewall under the CIS Controls framework may include the number of unmanaged devices detected, the percentage of employees who completed cybersecurity training, and the reduction in incident rates related to specific controls.

ISO 27001:

* *Framework Overview:* ISO/IEC 27001 is a globally recognized standard for information security management systems. It encompasses a systematic approach to managing information security risks.

* *Metrics:* Metrics under ISO 27001 can include the number of non-compliance incidents, the number of security awareness training sessions conducted, and the percentage of employees who participated in simulated phishing exercises.

CMMI Cybermaturity Platform:

* *Framework Overview:* The Capability Maturity Model Integration (CMMI) for Cybermaturity is a framework that provides a structured approach to assessing an organization's cybersecurity maturity.

* *Metrics:* Organizations can use CMMI metrics to track progress in enhancing employee awareness, improving access controls, reducing vulnerabilities, and responding effectively to incidents.

Human-Focused Metrics:

Metrics Overview: In addition to using established frameworks, organizations can develop custom metrics tailored to human-focused security efforts. These metrics can measure the effectiveness of awareness training, phishing simulations, and incident response.

Examples of Human-Focused Metrics:

* *Phishing click rates:* The percentage of employees who fell for simulated phishing attacks.

* *Incident response time*: The average time it takes to detect, respond to, and mitigate security incidents.

* *Training effectiveness:* The percentage of employees who demonstrate improved cybersecurity awareness and behavior after training.

Balanced Scorecard:

* *Framework Overview:* The Balanced Scorecard is a strategic framework that can be adapted to assess the effectiveness of human firewall efforts. It uses a balanced set of financial, customer, internal process, and learning and growth metrics.

* *Metrics:* Metrics related to the human firewall in a Balanced Scorecard approach may include employee satisfaction with training, the reduction in security incidents, and cost savings from improved security practices.

Maturity Models:

* *Framework Overview:* Organizations can adopt cybersecurity maturity models like the Cybersecurity Capability Maturity Model (C2M2) or the NIST Cybersecurity Framework's Implementation Tiers.

* *Metrics:* These models often provide maturity levels or stages with associated metrics for each stage. These metrics can help organizations assess their progress in strengthening the human firewall and improving overall cybersecurity posture.

When assessing the effectiveness of efforts to strengthen the human firewall, organizations should use a combination of qualitative and quantitative metrics to gain a comprehensive view of their cybersecurity posture. Regular measurement and continuous improvement are crucial to adapt to evolving threats and challenges.

Emerging Trends and Challenges In Human-centric Cybersecurity

Emerging trends and challenges in human-centric cybersecurity have gained prominence as organizations strive to protect their digital assets, especially in the context of remote work and evolving workplace dynamics. Two significant aspects of this evolving landscape are the use of AI and machine learning for threat detection and response, as well as the impact of remote work on the human firewall. Let's explore these aspects in detail:

1. **AI and Machine Learning for Threat Detection and Response:**

   Artificial Intelligence (AI) and Machine Learning (ML) have rapidly advanced in recent years and are increasingly being integrated into cybersecurity strategies. These technologies enable organizations to enhance their threat detection and response capabilities by processing large volumes of data, identifying patterns, and automating actions to counter cyber threats.

Challenges:

1. *False Positives and Negatives:* AI and ML algorithms, while powerful, are not infallible. They can produce false positives (flagging benign activities as threats) and false negatives (failing to detect actual threats). Organizations must continually fine-tune their algorithms to reduce these errors.

2. *Adversarial AI:* Cybercriminals are using AI to create sophisticated attacks that can evade traditional security measures. This cat-and-mouse game between AI-driven attacks and AI-driven defenses presents an ongoing challenge.

3. *Privacy and Ethics:* The use of AI and ML in cybersecurity raises ethical questions about privacy and data protection. Striking a balance between effective threat detection and preserving individuals' privacy is a challenge.

4. *Skill Gap:* The effective use of AI and ML in cybersecurity requires specialized skills. Organizations may face a shortage of cybersecurity professionals with expertise in these areas.

2. Impact of Remote Work and Evolving Workplace Dynamics on the Human Firewall:

The COVID-19 pandemic accelerated the shift towards remote work, which has become a fundamental aspect of the modern workplace. This trend has brought about significant changes in the way organizations manage their human firewalls.

Challenges:

1. *Increased Attack Surface:* Remote work has expanded an organization's attack surface, making it more challenging to defend. Home networks may lack the same level of security as corporate networks, and remote employees may not always adhere to the same security practices.

2. *Phishing and Social Engineering:* Cybercriminals are increasingly exploiting the emotional and psychological aspects of remote work, using phishing attacks related to COVID-19, remote collaboration tools, and pandemic-related concerns. The human element is more vulnerable to such tactics when working in isolation.

3. *Employee Burnout:* Remote work, while offering flexibility, can lead to burnout and reduced vigilance. Employees may be juggling personal and professional responsibilities, making them more susceptible to security lapses.

4. *Insider Threats:* Managing insider threats in remote work settings can be complex. Employees working remotely may feel isolated, and the lack of in-person oversight can create opportunities for malicious actions.

5. *Security Awareness Training:* Ensuring that remote employees receive adequate security awareness training and understand the unique risks associated with remote work is a challenge. Training programs need to be adapted to the remote work context.

6. *Collaboration Tools Security:* The rapid adoption of remote collaboration tools introduced new security challenges. Organizations need to secure these tools to prevent unauthorized access, data leaks, and other threats.

7. *Device Management:* Managing and securing a diverse range of devices used for remote work is a significant challenge. Organizations need to ensure that these devices are adequately patched and protected.

8. *Regulatory Compliance:* Remote work may introduce regulatory compliance challenges, particularly with regard to data protection and privacy regulations. Ensuring that remote work practices adhere to these regulations is vital.

9. *Maintaining a Security-Aware Culture:* Fostering a security-aware culture in a remote work environment requires different strategies. Organizations must encourage remote employees to take responsibility for security without physical oversight.

The strength of an organization's human firewall remains a cornerstone of its cybersecurity strategy. By recognizing the importance of the human factor and employing a multifaceted approach, organizations can better defend against threats, maintain regulatory compliance, and safeguard their reputation and assets in the digital age.

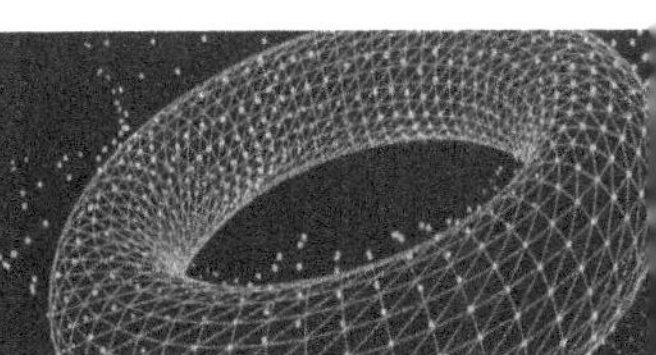

Behavioral Biases: How Cognitive Shortcuts Impact Risk Assessments.

Introduction to Cognitive Biases and Risk Assessment

In GRC, the human element plays a pivotal role in shaping decisions and strategies. Within this context, one of the most compelling and intricate aspects of human behavior is the influence of cognitive biases on risk assessments.

As we continue on this journey, we must acknowledge that our perception of risks, vulnerabilities, and compliance challenges is not purely rational. Our minds are susceptible to cognitive shortcuts and biases that can inadvertently distort our judgment. This chapter, "Behavioral Biases: How Cognitive Shortcuts Impact Risk Assessments," takes us deep into the psychology of decision-making and explores the profound implications of these biases on the GRC landscape.

Cognitive biases are the unconscious mental shortcuts that humans employ to process information and make decisions. While these biases can be helpful in simplifying complex situations, they can also lead to systematic errors in judgment. In the realm of GRC, where effective risk assessment is a cornerstone of sound decision-making, understanding how these biases influence our perception of risks is paramount.

In the chapters that follow, we will uncover the fascinating array of cognitive biases that can subtly shape our approach to risk assessments. From confirmation bias to availability heuristic and beyond, we will explore their impact on GRC processes and unveil real-world examples of how these biases have, at times, steered organizations off course.

However, this chapter is not merely about exposing the pitfalls of cognitive biases. It is about equipping GRC professionals with the knowledge, tools, and strategies to mitigate their influence. We will delve into best practices for conducting risk assessments that account for these biases, emphasizing the role of awareness, training, and organizational culture in fostering more objective evaluations.

As we embark on this exploration of behavioral biases in risk assessment, we invite you to reflect on your own practices, challenge your assumptions, and engage in critical thinking. The journey "Beyond Checkboxes" is not merely a quest for compliance but a pursuit of a deeper understanding of the intricate interplay between the human element and the world of GRC.

DEFINING CENTRAL CONCEPTS: COGNITIVE BIASES AND RISK ASSESSMENT.

COGNITIVE BIASES

Cognitive biases are systematic, patterned deviations from rationality in human judgment and decision-making. These biases are deeply rooted in the way the human brain processes information, often resulting in predictable yet irrational judgment and choice patterns. While cognitive biases can serve as cognitive shortcuts, simplifying complex decision-making processes, they can also lead to significant errors in perception and decision-making. In the realm of GRC, understanding these biases is of paramount importance, as they can profoundly influence the risk assessment process, compliance decisions, and governance strategies.

In an article for Forbes, Perry Carpenter, Chief Evangelist & Strategy Officer KnowBe4, Inc. makes a salient point, "People are programmed to take certain shortcuts as they process information. These are known as heuristics, or "mental shortcuts that allow people to solve problems and make judgments quickly and efficiently. Most of the time that can be a good thing. The sum of all our previous experiences helps us determine how to respond as we experience new situations. But sometimes those automatic responses get us into trouble — often because of unconscious biases that cause us to react quickly without considering consequences."

TYPES OF COGNITIVE BIAS

CONFIRMATION BIAS

This cognitive bias involves the human tendency to seek, interpret, and remember information in a way that confirms preexisting beliefs or hypotheses. In the context of GRC, this bias can lead to a selective gathering of information, often overlooking or downplaying data that contradicts existing beliefs. For instance, a compliance officer exhibiting confirmation bias may disproportionately focus on data that supports the organization's existing compliance practices, potentially ignoring critical compliance risks that necessitate attention.

In GRC, confirmation bias can manifest in several ways and significantly impact decision-making:

1. *Selective Information Gathering*: GRC professionals who fall victim to confirmation bias tend to actively seek out information that aligns with their existing beliefs or assumptions. They may conduct research, analyze data, or engage in discussions with a predisposition to find evidence that supports their current stance. This selective information gathering can result in an incomplete or one-sided view of risks and compliance issues.

2. *Interpreting Information in a Biased Manner*: Even when exposed to neutral or balanced information, individuals influenced by confirmation bias have a propensity to interpret that information in a way that confirms their preexisting beliefs. In the context of GRC, this can lead to the misinterpretation of regulatory requirements or the potential impact of specific risks, skewing decision-making processes.

3. *Memory Biases*: Confirmation bias also influences memory. GRC professionals may remember information that supports their existing beliefs more readily than information that contradicts them. This can lead to an inaccurate and skewed recollection of past compliance incidents, risk assessments, or regulatory interpretations.

4. *Influence on Risk Assessments*: Confirmation bias can profoundly affect risk assessments in GRC. For instance, a compliance officer may hold the belief that certain compliance practices within the organization are robust and effective. When conducting a risk assessment, this bias may lead to an overemphasis on data and evidence that supports the belief in the effectiveness of these practices, potentially overlooking areas that require improvement.

5. *Risk Mitigation and Compliance Decisions*: GRC professionals influenced by confirmation bias may make compliance and risk management decisions that align with their existing beliefs, rather than what a more objective analysis would indicate. This can result in a misallocation of resources, with a disproportionate focus on addressing perceived compliance risks while potentially neglecting other, more important concerns.

6. *Reinforcement of Biases*: Over time, confirmation bias can reinforce preexisting beliefs. GRC professionals who consistently seek, interpret, and remember information that confirms their biases may become even more entrenched in their views, making it challenging to adopt alternative perspectives or make unbiased decisions.

AVAILABILITY HEURISTIC

This bias occurs when individuals rely on readily available information when making decisions, often overestimating the importance of information that is easily accessible or memorable. In GRC, the availability heuristic can lead to an overemphasis on recent or highly publicized risks. Compliance professionals might be more inclined to prioritize compliance measures based on recent, highly publicized regulatory actions, even if they are not the most significant compliance risks for their specific organization. This can have significant implications in GRC, where the availability of information plays a crucial role in assessing risks and making compliance decisions. The influence of availability heuristics extends to various areas of GRC. They include:

1. *Influence on Risk Assessment*: GRC professionals may disproportionately focus on risks that are more visible, memorable, or have recently garnered attention. This bias can lead to the overestimation of the importance of high-profile risks, even if they are relatively rare, while underestimating the significance of less conspicuous but potentially higher-impact compliance and risk management concerns.

   For example, if there has been a recent high-profile data breach that received widespread media coverage, GRC professionals may be more likely to prioritize data security risks in their assessments, even if other, less publicized compliance issues pose a greater threat to the organization's objectives.

2. *Recent Events' Influence*: The availability heuristic gives recent events a disproportionate influence on decision-making. GRC professionals may perceive events or compliance incidents that have occurred in the near past as more relevant or important, potentially causing them to allocate resources or make compliance decisions based on the recency of such events rather than a comprehensive risk analysis.

   For instance, a recent regulatory fine imposed on the organization for a compliance violation may lead GRC professionals to allocate significant resources to address that specific issue, even if there are other, less recent but equally high-priority compliance risks that demand attention.

3. *Media and Publicity Impact*: The media's role in highlighting specific compliance incidents or risks can significantly influence GRC professionals' perceptions. Information that receives extensive media coverage is more likely to be readily available in the minds of GRC professionals, potentially leading to the overemphasis of such risks in risk assessments.

   Media exposure can also lead to the magnification of risks. For example, a data breach reported in the news may be perceived as more common or significant than it actually is, leading to a skewed risk assessment.

4. *Neglect of Underlying Risks*: The availability heuristic can lead to the neglect of underlying and less visible risks. Risks that do not receive extensive media attention or have not occurred recently may be underestimated, potentially resulting in insufficient risk mitigation strategies.

   For example, GRC professionals may focus on implementing stringent data security measures following a widely publicized data breach while neglecting equally essential but less visible compliance risks, such as internal control weaknesses.

Mitigating the Availability Heuristic in GRC

Mitigating the availability heuristic in GRC is essential to ensure that risk assessments and compliance decisions are objective and well-informed. Some strategies to counteract the availability heuristic include:

Data-Driven Decision-Making: Emphasize the importance of data-driven decision-making and risk assessment. Encourage GRC professionals to rely on empirical data and objective evidence when evaluating risks.

Long-Term Perspective: Promote a long-term perspective in risk assessment. Encourage GRC professionals to consider historical trends and patterns, rather than focusing solely on recent events.

Diverse Data Sources: Encourage the use of diverse data sources and methodologies in risk assessment. GRC professionals should consider a wide range of information, not solely what is easily accessible or recently available.

Objective Analysis: Implement a process of objective analysis, where risks are evaluated based on a comprehensive examination of data, rather than the availability of information.

Independent Review: Seek independent reviews or audits of risk assessments to ensure that decisions are not unduly influenced by recent or highly publicized events.

ANCHORING BIAS

Anchoring bias arises when individuals anchor or rely too heavily on the first piece of information they encounter when making decisions. In GRC, anchoring can lead to the over- or underestimation of risks based on initial data points. Compliance officers might anchor their risk assessments based on historical compliance data, potentially leading to either underestimating or overestimating risks associated with new regulatory requirements.

1. **Impact on Risk Assessments:**

    Anchoring bias can significantly impact risk assessment processes. GRC professionals may anchor their risk assessments based on initial data points, which can result in skewed judgments and decisions:

    a. ***Overestimation of Risks:*** If a GRC professional encounters an initial risk assessment or estimate that suggests a high level of risk, they may anchor their subsequent risk assessments to this high level, overestimating the likelihood or potential impact of risks.

b. *Underestimation of Risks:* Conversely, if the initial data point indicates a low level of risk, GRC professionals may anchor their risk assessments to this lower level, potentially underestimating the true risks associated with certain compliance obligations or governance practices.

For instance, if an organization has experienced a significant compliance breach in the past, GRC professionals may anchor their risk assessments to the severity of that breach and allocate excessive resources to mitigating similar risks, potentially overlooking other, equally pressing compliance issues.

2. Influence on Compliance Decisions:

Anchoring bias can affect compliance decisions, particularly in the context of regulatory interpretations and enforcement actions. If the organization has previously interpreted a regulation in a particular way or faced regulatory enforcement with specific consequences, GRC professionals may anchor their future compliance decisions based on these past interpretations or actions, potentially leading to a less flexible and adaptable approach to compliance.

In a situation where a previous regulatory audit resulted in a specific fine for a compliance violation, GRC professionals may anchor future compliance decisions to the level of that fine, potentially neglecting the possibility of different regulatory interpretations or consequences.

3. Inertia and Inflexibility:

Anchoring bias can lead to decision-making inertia and inflexibility. Once GRC professionals anchor their decisions based on initial data or interpretations, they may be less inclined to reevaluate or adapt their decisions, even in the face of new information or changing circumstances.

4. **Impact on Governance Practices:**

In the world of governance practices, anchoring bias can lead to the establishment of practices or policies based on historical decisions or circumstances. If a particular governance practice was implemented in response to a past governance challenge, GRC professionals may anchor their approach to future governance practices based on this historical reference point, potentially overlooking the need for evolving governance strategies.

MITIGATING ANCHORING BIAS IN GRC

Mitigating anchoring bias in GRC is essential to ensure that risk assessments, compliance decisions, and governance practices remain objective, adaptable, and well-informed. Some strategies to counteract anchoring bias include:

1. *Continuous Review*: Implement a process of continuous review and reevaluation of risk assessments, compliance decisions, and governance practices to prevent the anchoring of decisions based on past references.

2. *Flexibility and Adaptability*: Encourage flexibility and adaptability in GRC practices. GRC professionals should be open to reevaluating and adapting decisions in light of new information and changing circumstances.

3. *Objective Data Analysis:* Focus on objective data analysis and empirical evidence when making risk assessments and compliance decisions. Emphasize data-driven decision-making.

4. *Multiple Reference Points:* Encourage GRC professionals to consider multiple reference points and perspectives when making decisions, rather than relying solely on a single initial data point.

5. *Independent Review:* Seek independent reviews or audits of risk assessments and compliance decisions to ensure that decisions are not unduly anchored to past references.

OVERCONFIDENCE BIAS

This bias results in individuals overestimating their own abilities or the accuracy of their judgments. In GRC, overconfidence can lead to underestimating risks and compliance violations. A compliance officer who is overconfident in their understanding of complex regulatory requirements may overlook nuanced compliance risks, potentially exposing the organization to compliance violations.

1. **Impact on Compliance and Risk Assessment:**

   The overconfidence bias can significantly impact compliance and risk assessment processes through:

   a. *Underestimation of Compliance Risks*: GRC professionals influenced by overconfidence may underestimate the complexity and depth of compliance risks. This can lead to a lack of thorough analysis and risk assessments that do not adequately account for the nuances of compliance requirements.

   b. *Overemphasis on Known Risks:* Those affected by overconfidence bias may focus extensively on compliance risks or risk factors they feel they understand well, potentially neglecting less familiar but equally pivotal risk elements.

   Take as an example, a compliance officer may overestimate their grasp of complex data privacy regulations, leading to an underestimation of the organization's risk exposure in this area while dedicating disproportionate resources to addressing other, well-understood compliance risks.

2. Inaccurate Regulatory Interpretations:

Overconfidence bias can lead to the development of inaccurate regulatory interpretations. GRC professionals may believe they have a complete understanding of regulatory requirements, potentially leading to misguided interpretations and the implementation of compliance practices that do not align with the true spirit and intent of the regulations.

3. Suboptimal Decision-Making:

Overconfidence can result in suboptimal decision-making, as GRC professionals may believe they have all the answers and do not seek input from others. This can lead to an absence of diverse perspectives and the potential neglect of decisive governance practices or compliance strategies.

4. Resistance to Feedback:

GRC professionals influenced by overconfidence bias may be resistant to feedback or close evaluation of their decisions or practices. This can lead to a lack of continuous improvement in GRC practices, as they may believe their strategies are flawless.

5. Legal and Reputational Consequences:

Overconfidence bias can have significant legal and reputational consequences. When GRC professionals make decisions that are overly confident but incorrect, it can result in regulatory violations, fines, legal actions, and reputational damage for the organization.

MITIGATING OVERCONFIDENCE BIAS IN GRC

Mitigating overconfidence bias in GRC is crucial to ensure that compliance, risk assessment, and governance decisions remain objective, well-informed, and adaptable. Some strategies to counteract overconfidence bias include:

1. *Diverse Teams:* Encourage diverse teams in GRC departments to provide a range of perspectives and expertise. This diversity can help challenge overconfident views and promote a more holistic approach to decision-making.

2. *Objective Analysis:* Promote objective data analysis and empirical evidence when making compliance and risk assessment decisions. Emphasize data-driven decision-making over subjective judgments.

3. *Seek External Input:* Encourage GRC professionals to seek external input, such as third-party audits or regulatory consultations, to ensure regulatory interpretations are accurate and unbiased.

4. *Openness to Feedback:* Cultivate a culture of openness to feedback and continuous improvement in GRC practices. GRC professionals should actively seek and value constructive feedback from colleagues and external sources.

5. *Regular Review:* Implement a process of regular review and evaluation of compliance practices, risk assessments, and governance decisions to ensure they align with evolving compliance requirements and risk landscapes.

RECENCY BIAS

The recency bias entails giving more weight to recent events or information when making decisions. In the context of GRC, this can lead to a focus on recent incidents while neglecting historical risks. For example, a recent data breach may lead an organization to allocate excessive resources to data security while overlooking others.

1. **Impact on Risk Assessments:**

   Recency bias can significantly impact risk assessments in GRC through:

   a. *Overemphasis on Recent Events*: GRC professionals influenced by recency bias may place a disproportionate focus on recent events, even if they are relatively rare or not representative of long-term trends. This can lead to the overestimation of the importance of risks associated with recent incidents, potentially diverting resources from addressing other, less recent but equally critical compliance and risk management concerns.

   b. *Neglect of Historical Trends*: The bias can result in the neglect of historical trends and data. GRC professionals may overlook risk factors or compliance issues that are not currently in the spotlight, potentially leading to underestimation of these risks.

   For example, if there has been a recent high-profile data breach, GRC professionals may allocate substantial resources to address data security risks, potentially neglecting other, less recent but equally critical compliance risks, such as internal control weaknesses.

2. **Influence on Compliance Decisions:**

   Recency bias can affect compliance decisions, particularly in the interpretation and response to regulatory changes or enforcement actions. If there has been a recent regulatory change or enforcement action, GRC professionals may overemphasize the importance of these events and anchor their future compliance decisions based on these recent references.

For example, if a new regulation has been introduced or a regulatory authority has recently imposed a significant fine for a compliance violation, GRC professionals may prioritize these recent events in their compliance strategies, potentially overlooking other, equally critical compliance obligations.

3. **Short-Term Focus:**

   Recency bias can lead to a short-term focus in decision-making. GRC professionals may be more inclined to react to immediate and recent events, potentially neglecting the long-term impact of compliance practices and risk management strategies.

4. **Inconsistent Risk Prioritization:**

   GRC professionals influenced by recency bias may prioritize risks inconsistently. Recent events or data can carry more weight in risk prioritization, potentially leading to an unbalanced focus on certain risk factors at the expense of others.

MITIGATING RECENCY BIAS IN GRC

Mitigating recency bias in GRC is essential to ensuring that risk assessments, compliance strategies, and governance practices remain objective, well-informed, and adaptable. Some strategies to counteract recency bias include:

1.   *Long-Term Perspective*: Promote a long-term perspective in GRC practices. GRC professionals should consider historical trends and data when making risk assessments and compliance decisions, rather than solely focusing on recent events.

2.   *Objective Data Analysis:* Emphasize objective data analysis and empirical evidence when making compliance and risk assessment decisions. Encourage data-driven decision-making over subjective judgments.

3.   *Comprehensive Risk Assessment:* Encourage comprehensive risk assessments that take into account both recent and historical risk factors. Consider the full scope of potential risks rather than giving undue weight to recent events.

4.   *Diverse Data Sources:* Utilize diverse data sources and methodologies in risk assessments to ensure a balanced and holistic view of risk factors.

5.   *Continuous Review:* Implement a process of continuous review and evaluation of compliance practices, risk assessments, and governance decisions to adapt to evolving compliance requirements and risk landscapes.

HINDSIGHT BIAS

Hindsight bias involves perceiving past events as having been more predictable than they actually were. In GRC, hindsight bias can lead to misjudging past risk assessments and compliance decisions, potentially resulting in a lack of preparation for future risks.

1.   **Impact on Risk Assessments:**

     Hindsight bias can impact risk assessments in GRC by:

     a.   *Misjudging Past Risks*: GRC professionals influenced by hindsight bias may misjudge past risks and believe that they should have been able to predict and prepare for them. This bias can result in the belief that past risk assessments were more accurate and comprehensive than they were.

b. *Delayed Response to Emerging Risks*: The perception that past events were more predictable can lead to a delayed response to emerging risks. GRC professionals may believe they were adequately prepared for similar situations in the past, potentially neglecting the need for proactive risk mitigation.

If, for instance, an organization has experienced a cybersecurity breach, hindsight bias may lead GRC professionals to believe they should have known the breach was imminent, potentially delaying the implementation of additional security measures to prevent future breaches.

2.   Influence on Compliance Decisions:

Hindsight bias can affect compliance decisions, particularly in regulatory interpretations and enforcement actions. If an organization has previously faced regulatory actions, GRC professionals may believe they should have predicted those actions and could have taken steps to avoid them.

An instance is if a regulatory audit resulted in a fine for a compliance violation, hindsight bias may lead GRC professionals to believe they should have foreseen the regulatory violation, potentially neglecting the possibility of different regulatory interpretations or enforcement actions in the future.

3.   Inaccurate Assessment of Governance Practices:

Hindsight bias can lead to an inaccurate assessment of governance practices. GRC professionals may perceive past governance practices as being more effective and suitable than they actually were, potentially resisting changes and improvements.

4. **Influence on Decision-Making:**

   Hindsight bias can influence decision-making by leading GRC professionals to base decisions on the belief that past events were more predictable than they actually were. This can result in decisions that are not aligned with objective risk assessments and compliance requirements.

5. **Resistance to Feedback:**

   GRC professionals influenced by hindsight bias may be resistant to feedback or close evaluation of their decisions or practices. This can lead to a lack of continuous improvement in GRC practices, as they may believe their strategies were adequate in hindsight.

MITIGATING HINDSIGHT BIAS IN GRC

Mitigating hindsight bias in GRC is essential to ensure that risk assessments, compliance decisions, and governance practices remain objective, well-informed, and adaptable. Some strategies to counteract hindsight bias include:

1. *Objective Data Analysis:* Emphasize objective data analysis and empirical evidence when making compliance and risk assessment decisions. Encourage data-driven decision-making over subjective judgments.

2. *Long-Term Perspective:* Promote a long-term perspective in GRC practices. GRC professionals should consider historical trends and patterns, rather than believing that past events were more predictable than they actually were.

3. *Diverse Data Sources:* Utilize diverse data sources and methodologies in risk assessments to ensure a balanced view of risk factors and compliance obligations.

4. *Openness to Feedback:* Cultivate a culture of openness to feedback and continuous improvement in GRC practices. GRC professionals should actively seek and value constructive feedback from colleagues and external sources.

5. *Continuous Review:* Implement a process of continuous review and evaluation of compliance practices, risk assessments, and governance decisions to adapt to evolving compliance requirements and risk landscapes.

Understanding these cognitive biases is fundamental in GRC, as they can make or mar decision-making processes. Recognizing when these biases come into play is crucial for more objective and well-informed risk assessments and compliance practices.

THE RELEVANCE OF COGNITIVE BIASES IN GRC

Cognitive biases are highly relevant in the field of GRC due to their pervasive influence on decision-making processes. GRC professionals are tasked with ensuring that organizations maintain effective governance, manage risks, and remain compliant with relevant laws and regulations. In this context, cognitive biases can introduce substantial challenges and consequences:

* *Biased Risk Assessments*: Cognitive biases can distort risk assessments, leading to the overestimation or underestimation of certain risks. For instance, the confirmation bias may cause compliance professionals to favor information that confirms their preexisting beliefs about compliance risks, potentially overlooking paramount issues.

* *Misallocation of Resources*: Biases like the availability heuristic can lead to a disproportionate focus on risks that are more visible or memorable, potentially diverting

resources from more significant, but less conspicuous, compliance and risk management priorities.

* *Compliance Violations*: Cognitive biases can cloud judgment and lead to suboptimal compliance decisions. The overconfidence bias, for example, can result in overestimating one's understanding of complex regulations, potentially resulting in compliance violations.

* *Lack of Objectivity:* Biases can compromise the objectivity of GRC professionals, which is crucial for making sound decisions and maintaining impartiality in compliance and risk management efforts. For example, anchoring bias may lead to decisions anchored in initial data points rather than objective assessment.

* *Regulatory and Legal Implications*: Cognitive biases can have significant regulatory and legal consequences. When organizations make compliance decisions influenced by biases, they may inadvertently violate regulatory requirements, leading to fines, legal actions, and reputational damage.

* *Reputational Risks*: Biased decisions can negatively impact an organization's reputation. If a compliance or governance decision is perceived as being influenced by cognitive biases, it can erode trust among stakeholders, such as customers, partners, and investors.

HOW COGNITIVE BIASES IMPACT DECISION-MAKING IN GRC

1. *Selective Information Processing*: Cognitive biases influence the way GRC professionals gather and process information. Confirmation bias, for example, leads to a tendency to seek out information that confirms existing beliefs while ignoring contradictory data. In GRC, this can result in skewed risk assessments and compliance decisions.

2. *Inaccurate Risk Perception*: Cognitive biases can lead to inaccurate risk perception. The availability heuristic makes recent or vivid events more salient, potentially leading to the overemphasis of recent, high-profile compliance breaches, while overlooking less publicized but equally critical compliance risks.

3. *Inconsistent Risk Prioritization*: GRC professionals may prioritize risks inconsistently due to biases. Anchoring bias can lead to decisions anchored in initial data points, rather than a comprehensive risk analysis, potentially skewing risk prioritization.

4. *Overconfidence in Decision-Making*: The overconfidence bias can lead to an unwarranted belief in the accuracy of one's own judgments. In GRC, this overconfidence can lead to suboptimal risk assessment and compliance decisions.

5. *Delayed Response to Emerging Risks*: Hindsight bias can lead to the perception that past events were more predictable than they actually were. This can result in a delayed response to emerging risks, as organizations may believe they were adequately prepared for similar situations in the past.

6. *Inadequate Mitigation Strategies*: Cognitive biases can affect the development of risk mitigation strategies. GRC professionals may focus on addressing perceived high-impact risks while overlooking latent, lower-priority risks.

7. *Biased Compliance Practices*: Compliance practices, from regulatory interpretations to policy development, can be influenced by biases. This may lead to decisions that do not align with the true spirit and intent of regulatory requirements.

Real-life Case-Studies and Examples of How Cognitive Biases Influence GRC

Cognitive biases have a far-reaching effect across the board in GRC. This is simply because humans are in charge of taking important decisions in the day to day running of different organizations. Irrespective of industry, cognitive bias can come into play in various forms. Despite the loss or damages that may come from the influence of cognitive biases on decision making processes, they also provide a great opportunity to learn ways future mistakes can be avoided.

Let's take a look at some real-life cases of how cognitive bias has occurred in the past in a few industries;

1. *Enron and Overconfidence Bias*:

   Industry: Energy and Finance

   Case Study: The Enron scandal in the early 2000s is a classic example of overconfidence bias influencing GRC practices. Enron's executives displayed unwarranted confidence in their ability to manage complex financial structures and manipulate financial statements. This overconfidence led to a lack of critical assessment of the risks and compliance issues associated with these practices. Ultimately, the company collapsed due to fraudulent accounting practices and unethical behavior.

2. **2008 Financial Crisis and Hindsight Bias:**

   Industry: Finance

   Case Study: The 2008 financial crisis is an example of hindsight bias influencing GRC practices. Leading up to the crisis, many financial institutions and regulators exhibited hindsight bias by downplaying the risks associated with complex financial instruments, such as mortgage-backed securities. They believed that past economic stability should have signaled the predictability of the financial system's health. This bias contributed to the underestimation of systemic risks and inadequate regulatory oversight.

3. **Volkswagen Emissions Scandal and Confirmation Bias:**

Industry: Automotive

Case Study: The Volkswagen emissions scandal is a prime example of confirmation bias affecting GRC practices. Volkswagen engineers and executives held a belief that their diesel engines met emission standards. They actively sought evidence that confirmed their preconceived notion while overlooking contradictory data. This confirmation bias led to the intentional manipulation of emissions tests to meet regulatory requirements.

4. **Equifax Data Breach and Availability Heuristic:**

Industry: Credit and Data Management

Case Study: The Equifax data breach in 2017 demonstrates the influence of the availability heuristic on GRC practices. Equifax's leadership may have overemphasized the significance of protecting consumer data due to the readily available examples of other high-profile data breaches. This led to an underestimation of the risks associated with inadequate cybersecurity practices, ultimately resulting in a massive data breach.

5. **Wells Fargo Unauthorized Account Openings and Anchoring Bias:**

Industry: Banking

Case Study: The Wells Fargo unauthorized account openings scandal showcases anchoring bias affecting GRC practices. The bank's employees were incentivized to open a certain number of accounts, which led to an overemphasis on achieving specific sales targets. This anchoring to sales targets overshadowed compliance obligations and ethical considerations, resulting in millions of unauthorized accounts being opened.

6. **Boeing 737 MAX Crashes and Recency Bias:**

Industry: Aerospace

Case Study: The Boeing 737 MAX crashes provide an example of recency bias impacting GRC practices. After years of safe flight records, Boeing may have fallen victim to recency bias by underestimating the significance of design and software issues that were contributing factors to the crashes. Recent success with previous aircraft models led to a short-term focus on profit and schedule over safety.

7. *Toyota Unintended Acceleration Recall and Anchoring Bias:*

Industry: Automotive

Case Study: The Toyota unintended acceleration recall is an example of anchoring bias in GRC practices. Toyota initially anchored their response to isolated reports of unintended acceleration issues, leading them to believe the problem was limited in scope. This bias delayed a comprehensive response and recall, resulting in a more extensive problem than initially perceived.

8. **Volkswagen Emissions Scandal (Part II) and Overconfidence Bias:**

Industry: Automotive

Case Study: The Volkswagen emissions scandal also illustrates overconfidence bias. After the initial discovery of emissions cheating, Volkswagen's leadership displayed overconfidence by underestimating the potential legal and financial consequences. This bias delayed a more comprehensive and transparent response, increasing the overall damage to the company.

9. **9. Facebook's Data Privacy Issues and Recency Bias:**

Industry: Technology and Social Media

Case Study: Facebook's data privacy issues, including the Cambridge Analytica scandal, exemplify the impact of recency bias. Despite concerns about data privacy over the years, Facebook exhibited recency bias by underestimating the potential regulatory and reputational risks associated with recent data breaches. This bias influenced their response and regulatory compliance.

10. **BP Deepwater Horizon Oil Spill and Hindsight Bias:**

Industry: Energy

Case Study: The BP Deepwater Horizon oil spill is an example of hindsight bias in GRC practices. Prior to the disaster, BP may have displayed hindsight bias by underestimating the likelihood of a catastrophic blowout. After the spill, they recognized the disaster as more predictable in hindsight, which influenced their subsequent risk assessments and safety measures.

11. **Volkswagen's Compliance with ESG Standards and Confirmation Bias:**

Industry: Automotive

Case Study: Volkswagen's efforts to comply with environmental, social, and governance (ESG) standards can demonstrate confirmation bias. In the aftermath of the emissions scandal, Volkswagen may seek out and emphasize information and reports that support their commitment to ESG standards to confirm their commitment to environmental responsibility, potentially downplaying ongoing compliance challenges.

RISK ASSESSMENT

Risk assessment, within the context of GRC, is a structured and systematic process aimed at identifying, evaluating, and prioritizing potential risks and threats that an organization may face. It involves a comprehensive analysis of vulnerabilities, threats, and the potential impact of risks on an organization's objectives, operations, and compliance obligations.

THE KEY COMPONENTS OF RISK ASSESSMENT WITHIN GRC INCLUDE:

1. *Risk Identification:* This phase involves identifying and cataloging potential risks faced by the organization. These risks encompass a wide array, including compliance risks, security risks, operational risks, financial risks, and more. It is essential to identify both internal and external risks that could affect the organization's ability to meet its objectives.

2. *Risk Analysis:* After the identification phase, organizations delve into the analysis of identified risks. This analysis aims to assess the likelihood of a risk occurring and its potential impact. This key step allows for the prioritization of risks for further assessment and mitigation efforts.

3. *Risk Evaluation:* In this stage, risks are evaluated based on their significance to the organization. This evaluation involves assessing the potential consequences of a risk and determining its importance within the context of the organization's objectives and compliance requirements. Risks are often categorized and prioritized based on their evaluation.

4. *Risk Mitigation:* Once risks are evaluated, organizations develop strategies to mitigate, avoid, transfer, or accept them. Risk mitigation strategies aim to reduce the impact or likelihood of a risk occurring. These strategies can encompass various measures, from implementing security controls to ensuring compliance with regulatory requirements.

5. *Monitoring and Review:* Risk assessment is not a one-time process but an ongoing one. Organizations continually monitor and review their risk assessments to ensure they remain up-to-date and relevant. This includes adapting to changing compliance requirements, emerging threats, and evolving business objectives.

Risk assessment provides a structured approach to understanding and addressing the risks that could impact an organization's ability to achieve its objectives and maintain compliance with legal and regulatory obligations. Effective risk assessment within GRC accounts for both the potential impact of risks and the influence of cognitive biases on decision-making processes. It is a dynamic and iterative process that ensures organizations remain proactive in identifying and managing risks that may hinder their compliance, governance, and risk management objectives.

BEST PRACTICES FOR CONDUCTING RISK ASSESSMENT THAT ACCOUNTS FOR COGNITIVE BIASES

Now that we have identified that cognitive biases can and will always be an issue organizations need to deal with, it is imperative that we also look at best practices for limiting the effect it has on risk assessment to engender better outcomes. This is to ensure that your organization's GRC practices are objective, well-informed and effective.

Here's a comprehensive set of best practices you can apply;

1. **Diverse and Inclusive Teams**

   Assemble diverse teams with varied backgrounds, perspectives, and expertise to participate in risk assessments. Different viewpoints can help counterbalance individual biases and provide a more holistic view of risks.

2. **Define Clear Objectives**

   Clearly define the objectives of the risk assessment to maintain focus and avoid scope creep, which can be influenced by cognitive biases.

3. **Structured Data Collection**

   Use structured data collection methods to ensure that information is gathered in an unbiased manner. This reduces the likelihood of cherry-picking data that aligns with preconceived notions.

4. **Data Validation**

   Regularly validate data used in risk assessments to ensure its accuracy, reliability, and relevance. Biased data can lead to biased assessments.

5. **Continuous Training**

   Provide ongoing training for GRC professionals to increase their awareness of cognitive biases and to develop strategies for mitigating them in decision-making.

6. **External Audits**

   Seek external audits or reviews of your risk assessments to gain an independent perspective and reduce the influence of internal biases.

7. **Scenario Planning**

   Incorporate scenario planning into risk assessments. Consider a range of potential scenarios, both likely and unlikely, to prevent over-reliance on certain assumptions.

8. **Utilize Technology**

   Leverage technology, such as risk management software, to automate data collection and analysis. This can help remove some human biases from the process.

9. **Blind Reviews**

   Implement blind reviews of risk assessments, where reviewers do not have access to the names or affiliations of the individuals who conducted the assessment. This can help reduce bias related to the source of the assessment.

10. **Balanced Metrics**

    Avoid overemphasizing certain metrics or indicators that are readily available. Ensure that a wide range of relevant metrics is considered to prevent the influence of availability or anchoring biases.

11. **Stakeholder Involvement**

    Include input from a broad spectrum of stakeholders, including employees, customers, regulators, and other relevant parties. Diverse input can provide a more comprehensive view of risks.

12. **Red Team Exercises**

    Conduct red team exercises, where a group of individuals deliberately takes on the role of challenging the assumptions and conclusions of the risk assessment. This can help identify and address confirmation bias.

13. **Independent Risk Oversight**

    Establish an independent risk oversight function that operates separately from day-to-day GRC functions to ensure that assessments are unbiased.

14. Benchmarking

Use benchmarking and industry comparisons to gain an external perspective on the validity and accuracy of your risk assessments.

15. Reporting Transparency

Maintain transparency in reporting by clearly documenting the methodologies, assumptions, and data sources used in the risk assessment process. This enables external stakeholders to assess the assessment's validity.

16. Adaptive Approach

Recognize that risk assessments are not static and should be subject to continuous review and updates. Cognitive biases may change over time, so staying adaptable is crucial.

17. Feedback Mechanisms

Establish feedback mechanisms that allow for regular input from employees and stakeholders on the effectiveness of risk assessments. This feedback can help identify and mitigate biases.

18. Document Decision-Making

A process that is well documented is not only valuable in the present but in the future as well. Document the decision-making process during risk assessments, including the reasoning behind choices made. This documentation can serve as a valuable reference point for future assessments and reduce the impact of hindsight bias.

AN OVERVIEW OF METHODOLOGIES FOR A MORE OBJECTIVE AND UNBIASED RISK EVALUATION

To achieve a more objective and unbiased risk evaluation in Governance, Risk Management and Compliance practices, it is necessary to utilize rigorous methodologies and processes. In this way, organizations can be sure that whatever decision they arrive at is well measured and calculated.

1. **Quantitative Risk Analysis**

    Utilize quantitative methods to assign numerical values to risks, such as probabilities, impacts, and frequencies. This approach enables the use of statistical tools to objectively assess and compare risks. Tools like Monte Carlo simulations can help model complex risk scenarios.

2. **Historical Data Analysis**

    Base risk evaluation on historical data and actual outcomes, rather than relying solely on subjective assessments. Analyze past incidents and their impact to identify trends and potential risks more objectively.

3. **Key Risk Indicators (KRIs)**

    Establish a set of key risk indicators that are monitored and measured regularly. KRIs provide a quantitative basis for assessing risk, helping to reduce cognitive biases related to the availability of information.

4. **Risk Matrices**

    Use risk matrices to visually map and rank risks based on predefined criteria. By establishing clear criteria for likelihood and impact, you can standardize the evaluation process and reduce subjectivity.

5. **Regulatory and Industry Standards**

    Refer to established regulatory and industry standards for risk evaluation and compliance. These standards often provide objective criteria for risk assessment and compliance obligations.

6. **Scenario Analysis**

    Develop and evaluate various scenarios to assess potential risks. Scenario analysis allows for a structured exploration of risks and their potential impacts, reducing bias related to confirmation and anchoring.

7. **Expert Panels and Delphi Method**

    Assemble expert panels to provide diverse perspectives on risk. The Delphi method, a structured and iterative approach to collecting and distilling expert opinions, can help eliminate individual biases.

8. **Risk Heat Maps**

    Use risk heat maps to visually represent risk levels across different categories. This method can help stakeholders quickly grasp the relative importance of risks.

9. **Risk Maturity Models**

    Implement risk maturity models to assess the organization's risk management practices objectively. These models provide benchmarks for the organization's risk management capabilities.

10. **Third-Party Assessments**

    Seek third-party assessments and audits to provide an independent evaluation of risk. External assessments can help mitigate internal biases and provide an unbiased perspective.

11. **Bayesian Networks**

    Employ Bayesian networks to model and analyze complex risk relationships. This approach allows for a structured assessment of dependencies and can help reduce subjective judgment.

12. Continuous Monitoring and Reporting

Implement continuous monitoring of key risk indicators and establish regular reporting mechanisms. This ongoing assessment helps ensure that risk evaluation remains objective and adapts to changing conditions.

13. Multivariate Analysis

Use multivariate statistical techniques to analyze multiple risk factors simultaneously. This approach allows for a more holistic understanding of risk relationships and can uncover hidden dependencies.

14. External Data Sources

Incorporate external data sources, such as market data, benchmarks, and industry reports, to provide an external perspective and reduce biases related to limited internal information.

15. Robotic Process Automation (RPA)

Consider RPA for routine risk assessment tasks to minimize human bias and errors. RPA can streamline data collection and analysis, ensuring consistency and objectivity.

16. Risk Analytics Platforms

Invest in advanced risk analytics platforms that can leverage machine learning and artificial intelligence to objectively assess and predict risks based on a broad range of data sources.

TRAINING AND EDUCATION: THE GRC PROFESSIONAL'S HACK TO STAYING AHEAD

Henry Ford once said "The only thing worse than training your employees and having them leave is not training them and having them stay." This holds true especially in GRC. An untrained employee is a disaster waiting to happen and it's just a matter of time.

Training and education has a pivotal role in shaping any organization's team's response to challenges at crucial times. It can make the difference between avoiding damages entirely and walking straight into the traps of cyber criminals.

Ongoing training for GRC professionals provides them with access to the right knowledge required at various times to ensure the security of data and systems.

There are several important reasons why continuous learning is paramount in this field and below are a few of them:

1. *Complex and Evolving Landscape*: The GRC landscape is characterized by its complexity and constant evolution. Regulations, industry standards, and best practices are continuously changing. Staying up to date with these developments is essential to ensure that your organization remains compliant and mitigates risks effectively.

2. *Diverse and Interrelated Domains*: GRC spans multiple domains, including governance, risk management, and compliance. GRC professionals need a broad skill set that covers legal, financial, technological, and operational aspects. Ongoing training helps individuals build and maintain expertise in each of these areas.

3. *Cognitive Bias Awareness*: Cognitive biases, which can affect decision-making, risk assessments, and compliance processes, are a significant challenge in GRC. Continuous training helps professionals recognize and mitigate these biases, leading to more objective and rational decision-making.

4. *Technology Advancements:* Technology plays a significant role in GRC, from risk assessment tools to compliance management software. Staying current with the latest technologies and understanding their implications is crucial for efficient GRC operations.

5. *Emerging Risks:* New risks continuously emerge in the business landscape. Ongoing education allows GRC professionals to identify and assess these risks promptly, enabling the organization to take proactive measures.

6. *Adherence to Ethical Standards:* GRC professionals often handle sensitive information and make vital decisions that impact the organization's reputation and stakeholders. Ongoing education helps maintain a strong ethical foundation, ensuring that professionals adhere to the highest standards of integrity and transparency.

7. *Regulatory Changes:* Regulatory changes can have a profound impact on an organization's GRC practices. Regular training helps GRC professionals interpret and implement these changes effectively, reducing the risk of compliance violations.

8. *Adaptation to Organizational Changes:* Organizations evolve, whether through mergers, acquisitions, structural changes, or expansions into new markets. GRC professionals must adapt to these changes, and ongoing training equips them with the necessary skills and knowledge.

9. *Stakeholder Expectations:* Stakeholders, including investors, customers, and regulators, have increasingly higher expectations for transparency and compliance. Continuous education helps GRC professionals meet these expectations and communicate effectively with stakeholders.

10. *Risk Mitigation:* Effective GRC relies on identifying and mitigating risks. Ongoing training helps professionals refine their risk assessment and management skills, leading to more comprehensive and accurate risk mitigation strategies.

11. *Professional Growth and Advancement:* GRC professionals who invest in ongoing training demonstrate a commitment to their field and their own professional development. This can open doors to career advancement and leadership roles within the organization.

12. *Resilience in Crisis Situations:* In times of crisis, such as a cybersecurity breach or a financial scandal, well-trained GRC professionals are better equipped to respond effectively and minimize the impact on the organization.

Training and Education in GRC can take various forms. From workshops, to simulations and case study analysis, these experiential learning methods provide practical, hands-on processes that can enhance understanding and recognition of cognitive biases. Adoption of one or all these methods will help improve overall performance on task if done correctly.

Let's take a closer look at how they contribute to bias awareness:

1. **Workshops:**

   Workshops are interactive and collaborative learning experiences where GRC professionals can actively engage with the topic of cognitive biases. Here's how workshops help improve bias awareness:

* *Active Participation:* Workshops encourage active participation, which helps participants apply theoretical knowledge to real-world scenarios, promoting a deeper understanding of biases.

* *Discussion and Sharing:* In workshops, participants can discuss their experiences and perspectives, allowing them to gain insights from others and become more aware of how biases may affect their decisions and actions.

* *Group Activities:* Collaborative exercises in workshops can demonstrate how group dynamics, such as groupthink or confirmation bias, impact decision-making processes. This helps participants recognize biases in a team setting.

* *Feedback and Reflection:* Workshops often include opportunities for feedback and reflection, enabling participants to assess their own decision-making and thought processes and identify potential biases.

* Practical Strategies: Workshops can introduce practical strategies and techniques for recognizing and mitigating cognitive biases in real-life GRC scenarios.

2. **Simulations:**

Simulations provide a controlled environment that replicates real-world situations. These activities immerse participants in scenarios where they must confront cognitive biases.

Here's how simulations contribute to bias awareness:

* *Experiential Learning:* Simulations allow participants to experience the consequences of biases firsthand, making the impact of these biases more tangible and memorable.

* *Risk-Free Environment:* **Participants can make decisions in a risk-free environment, enabling them to learn from mistakes and explore different responses to cognitive biases without real-world consequences.**

* *Complex Scenarios:* **Simulations can introduce complex scenarios that mimic the challenges GRC professionals face in their roles, highlighting the potential pitfalls of cognitive biases in decision-making.**

* *Immediate Feedback:* **Simulations often provide immediate feedback, allowing participants to see the consequences of their decisions and better understand how biases may have influenced their choices.**

* *Team Dynamics:* **Team-based simulations can illustrate how biases affect group decision-making processes, emphasizing the importance of recognizing and addressing biases in a collaborative setting.**

3. **Case Studies:**

Case studies present real or fictional scenarios in which cognitive biases played a role in significant events or decisions. Analyzing these cases helps GRC professionals identify biases and their consequences. Here's how case studies contribute to bias awareness:

a. *Real-World Relevance:* Case studies relate directly to practical GRC situations, making the recognition of biases in the workplace more relatable and relevant.

b. *Critical Analysis:* Participants can critically analyze the actions and decisions of individuals in the case study, allowing them to spot instances of cognitive biases.

c. *Pattern Recognition:* Case studies often reveal patterns in human behavior, which can help participants recognize common biases and their typical outcomes.

d. *Ethical Considerations:* Case studies often involve ethical dilemmas, prompting participants to reflect on the ethical dimensions of decision-making influenced by biases.

7Root Cause Analysis: Participants can trace the root causes of a particular event or decision, which may lead to the discovery of underlying cognitive biases that played a role

REGULATORY AND COMPLIANCE IMPLICATIONS

Just like any professional field of practice, there should be standards that must be strictly adhered to and consequences for defaulting if the highest form of professionalism is to be achieved.

Though specific compliance requirements may vary from industry to industry, when it comes to cognitive biases, there are quite a few similar instances where the lines may merge and issues can be addressed in a generic manner. Compliance processes are needed to address identified risks with appropriate risk elimination or reduction measures, PwC (2004)

Some ways in which regulatory bodies and compliance standards address the influence of cognitive biases on GRC practices include:

1. **Ethical Standards and Codes of Conduct:**

   Regulatory bodies often establish ethical standards and codes of conduct that emphasize objectivity, transparency, and ethical decision-making. These standards aim to reduce the impact of cognitive biases on GRC practices by promoting a strong ethical foundation.

2. **Reporting and Transparency:**

   Many compliance standards require organizations to maintain transparency in their GRC processes. This includes disclosing information about risk assessments, compliance efforts, and decision-making. Transparency can help identify and mitigate the influence of biases.

3. **Risk Assessment Guidelines:**

   Regulatory bodies and compliance standards provide guidelines and best practices for risk assessments. These guidelines often emphasize the need for unbiased, data-driven risk assessments to mitigate cognitive biases.

4. **Independent Oversight:**

   Some compliance standards mandate the presence of independent oversight in GRC processes. This oversight helps reduce the influence of internal biases by ensuring an external perspective on risk assessments and compliance decisions.

5. **Regulatory Examinations:**

   Regulatory bodies conduct examinations and audits to assess an organization's compliance with regulations and standards. These examinations can identify instances of bias and non-compliance with ethical standards.

6. **Reporting Requirements:**

   Compliance standards often mandate specific reporting requirements for risk assessments and compliance efforts. These requirements may include the need to document the methodologies used and the rationale behind decisions, which enhances transparency and accountability.

7. **Diversity and Inclusion Initiatives:**

   Some regulatory bodies and compliance standards promote diversity and inclusion as a means of mitigating bias. Encouraging diverse perspectives in GRC processes can help counteract the influence of cognitive biases.

8. **Ongoing Training and Education:**

   Regulatory bodies may require organizations to provide ongoing training and education for GRC professionals. These training programs often include elements related to bias awareness and mitigation.

9. **Whistleblower Protection:**

   Compliance standards may include provisions for whistleblower protection, allowing individuals to report instances of bias and misconduct without fear of retaliation.

10. **Evaluation of Compliance Programs:**

    Regulatory bodies assess the effectiveness of an organization's compliance program, which includes evaluating the steps taken to reduce the influence of cognitive biases on GRC practices.

11. **Benchmarking and Industry Comparisons:**

    Some compliance standards encourage organizations to benchmark their GRC practices against industry peers and best practices. This external perspective can help identify areas where biases may be affecting decision-making.

12. **Compliance Auditors and Consultants:**

    Compliance auditors and consultants may assist organizations in assessing and improving their GRC practices. They can provide an independent perspective on bias mitigation.

13. **Regulatory Sanctions and Enforcement:**

    Regulatory bodies have the authority to impose sanctions and enforcement actions on organizations that fail to address biases and non-compliance. This acts as a strong incentive for organizations to take bias mitigation seriously

LEGAL AND FINANCIAL CONSEQUENCES: THE COST OF FAILING TO ACCOUNT FOR BIASES IN RISK ASSESSMENTS.

Earlier, we pointed out that because there are standards that must be adhered to in the practice of GRC, there are also consequences for failure to comply. These consequences are usually either legal or financial. Just like in the real-life case studies we mentioned earlier, organizations end up with a scandal on their hands ultimately when biases go unchecked.

Let's discuss these consequences in detail:

1. **Legal Consequences:**

   a. **Regulatory Violations:**

      Regulatory bodies impose strict requirements on organizations to conduct unbiased and accurate risk assessments, especially in heavily regulated industries like finance, healthcare, and environmental protection. Failing to do so can lead to violations of these regulations.

   b. **Non-Compliance Penalties:**

      Non-compliance with regulatory requirements can result in penalties, fines, and legal actions. Regulatory bodies may impose substantial fines on organizations that are found to have conducted biased risk assessments, as it undermines the integrity of the regulatory framework.

   c. **Lawsuits and Legal Claims:**

      Biased risk assessments can lead to lawsuits from stakeholders, such as customers, investors, or employees, who may suffer harm due to inaccurate risk evaluations. These legal claims can result in costly settlements or court judgments against the organization.

d. **Reputational Damage:**

Legal consequences often come hand in hand with severe reputational damage. Organizations found guilty of conducting biased risk assessments may face public scrutiny, which can lead to a loss of trust from customers, investors, and the general public.

e. **Criminal Liability:**

In cases of egregious misconduct or fraud, individuals within the organization, particularly GRC professionals involved in risk assessments, may face criminal liability, including fines and imprisonment.

2. **Financial Consequences:**

a. *Financial Losses:*

Failing to account for biases can result in financial losses due to poor decision-making. Inaccurate risk assessments can lead to investments in high-risk ventures, regulatory fines, operational disruptions, and the misallocation of resources.

b. *Opportunity Costs:*

Biases in risk assessments can cause organizations to overlook profitable opportunities or overestimate the potential for profit. This can result in missed revenue or wasted resources.

c. *Increased Costs of Capital:*

Lenders and investors may perceive organizations with a history of biased risk assessments as higher risk. Consequently, they may charge higher interest rates or demand more significant returns on investment, increasing the cost of capital.

d. *Decreased Market Value:*

Repeated instances of biased risk assessments can lead to a decrease in the market value of an organization's stock or bonds. Shareholders and investors may respond negatively to the perceived increased risk.

e. *Loss of Competitive Advantage:*

Biased risk assessments can lead to poor strategic decisions, which may diminish an organization's competitive advantage and market position. Competitors who make more objective and informed decisions may gain an edge.

f. *Operational and Supply Chain Disruptions:*

Biased risk assessments may lead to incorrect risk prioritization, potentially resulting in operational disruptions, supply chain interruptions, or other unforeseen events that can be financially damaging.

g. *Higher Insurance Premiums:*

Insurers may adjust premium rates based on an organization's risk assessments. Biased assessments can lead to higher insurance costs, further impacting the financial bottom line.

h. *Litigation Costs:*

Legal consequences, such as lawsuits and regulatory investigations, can lead to significant litigation costs, including legal fees, settlements, and court-related expenses.

TRENDS AND EMERGING TECHNOLOGIES: THEIR IMPACT ON THE FUTURE OF COGNITIVE BIASES IN RISK ASSESSMENTS.

Emerging technologies, including Artificial Intelligence (AI) and Machine Learning (ML), have the potential to significantly reduce the impact of cognitive biases in risk assessments within the realm of Governance, Risk Management, and Compliance (GRC).

With the application of AI and ML, organizations are in a better position to enhance their capacity to manage risk assessment with lesser concern for biases.

These technologies can strengthen risk assessment through:

1. *Data-Driven Decision-Making:*

   AI and ML can analyze vast amounts of data to identify and assess risks without being influenced by human biases. By relying on objective data and algorithms, these technologies help ensure more impartial risk assessments.

2. *Pattern Recognition:*

   AI and ML are adept at recognizing patterns in data that may be overlooked by human assessors. This ability is particularly valuable in identifying emerging risks and subtle indicators of potential issues.

3. *Predictive Analytics:*

   These technologies can employ predictive analytics to forecast potential risks and their impact on an organization. By using historical data and various risk factors, AI and ML can provide more accurate predictions, minimizing the influence of cognitive biases.

4. ***Automated Decision-Making:***

AI can be used to automate routine and data-driven decision-making processes in GRC. This reduces the reliance on human judgment and minimizes the potential for cognitive biases to affect decisions.

5. ***Natural Language Processing (NLP):***

NLP capabilities in AI enable the extraction and analysis of textual data, such as compliance documents, regulations, and legal contracts. By automatically processing and categorizing this information, NLP can reduce the risk of misinterpretation or selective attention that cognitive biases may introduce.

6. ***Risk Modeling and Simulation:***

AI and ML can create complex risk models and simulations that account for various factors, including biases. By using these models, organizations can assess the potential impact of cognitive biases on decision-making and develop strategies to mitigate them.

7. ***Algorithmic Risk Assessment:***

AI algorithms can perform risk assessments using predefined rules and parameters. This process reduces the subjectivity introduced by cognitive biases and ensures that assessments are conducted consistently.

8. ***Continuous Monitoring:***

AI and ML can provide real-time monitoring of key risk indicators and compliance metrics. They can detect anomalies and deviations from established norms, reducing the risk of hindsight bias in post-event risk assessments.

9. ***Unbiased Data Collection and Analysis:***

   AI systems are trained to collect, process, and analyze data without inherent biases. This ensures that the data used in risk assessments is as objective and impartial as possible.

10. ***Customization and Adaptability:***

   AI and ML systems can be tailored to an organization's specific needs. They can adapt to evolving risks and changing circumstances, continuously improving the accuracy and objectivity of risk assessments.

11. ***Scenario Analysis:***

   AI can perform extensive scenario analysis by simulating various risk scenarios. This helps organizations explore the potential outcomes of different decisions without the interference of cognitive biases.

12. ***Oversight and Audit Trails:***

   AI systems can create detailed audit trails of risk assessments and decisions, providing transparency and accountability. This oversight reduces the risk of bias-driven decisions going unnoticed.

While AI and ML offer tremendous potential in reducing the impact of cognitive biases in risk assessments, it's important to acknowledge that these technologies are not entirely immune to bias themselves. The quality of data, the design of algorithms, and the training data can introduce their own biases. Therefore, it's essential to employ rigorous oversight and governance of AI and ML systems to ensure they remain objective and neutral.

HOW A DATA-DRIVEN APPROACH AND ADVANCED ANALYTICS ENHANCES OBJECTIVITY

In advocating for the use of artificial intelligence and machine learning, the outcome any organization should be aiming for is improved objectivity. With increased objectivity, there are lesser chances of cognitive biases interring in decision making processes.

By relying on empirical data and analytical methods, organizations can minimize the influence of cognitive bias. This can be achieved by:

1. ***Eliminating Subjectivity:***

   Data-driven approaches rely on factual data rather than subjective opinions. This eliminates the subjective and emotional factors that can introduce cognitive biases into decision-making processes. By basing assessments on objective data, GRC professionals can make more impartial and rational judgments.

2. ***Objectivity in Risk Assessment:***

   Risk assessments are central to GRC practices. Data-driven approaches employ advanced analytics to quantify and evaluate risks. This quantification reduces the likelihood of overestimating or underestimating risks based on personal biases. It provides a structured, data-driven foundation for decision-making.

3. ***Identifying Emerging Risks:***

   Advanced analytics, including predictive modeling and data mining, enable organizations to identify emerging risks early on. These techniques analyze historical and real-time data to identify patterns and anomalies, allowing organizations to proactively address risks without being influenced by hindsight bias.

4. ***Statistical Analysis:***

Statistical analysis is a key component of data-driven approaches. It provides a systematic method for analyzing data, identifying correlations, and making inferences. Statistical techniques help uncover hidden insights in data and reduce the impact of biases that may lead to incorrect conclusions.

5. ***Data Validation and Verification:***

Data-driven approaches emphasize the importance of data accuracy and validation. By thoroughly validating and verifying data sources, organizations can ensure the reliability of the information used in GRC assessments. This minimizes the impact of biases that may arise from using flawed or incomplete data.

6. ***Predictive Analytics:***

Predictive analytics leverages historical data to make informed forecasts about future events and trends. It reduces the reliance on personal judgment, intuition, or gut feeling, all of which can be influenced by cognitive biases. Predictive models help in making more objective predictions.

7. ***Machine Learning Algorithms:***

Machine learning algorithms can analyze vast datasets to identify patterns and relationships. These algorithms are not influenced by cognitive biases and can uncover insights that humans might miss. For example, they can detect unusual financial transactions indicative of fraud without the influence of confirmation bias.

8. ***Scenario Analysis:***

Advanced analytics can perform scenario analysis, where multiple scenarios and their potential impacts are evaluated. By objectively considering a range of possibilities, organizations reduce the risk of anchoring bias, which occurs when decisions are overly influenced by the first piece of information received.

9. ***Real-Time Monitoring:***

Data-driven approaches enable real-time monitoring of key risk indicators. This continuous monitoring allows organizations to detect anomalies and deviations promptly, reducing the risk of confirmation bias, as potential issues are identified and addressed in real-time.

10. ***Customization and Adaptability:***

Data-driven approaches can be customized to align with an organization's specific risk factors, industry standards, and objectives. This adaptability ensures that risk assessments remain relevant and objective, as they are tailored to the organization's unique needs.

11. ***Data-Backed Compliance:***

Compliance efforts benefit from data-driven approaches by using historical data to assess adherence to regulations and standards. This minimizes the impact of bias in compliance evaluations and ensures that organizations maintain their ethical and legal standing.

12. ***Audit Trails and Accountability:***

Data-driven processes often generate detailed audit trails, which provide transparency and accountability. These audit trails make it easier to track decision-making processes and hold individuals accountable for their actions, reducing the risk of hindsight bias.

CRITICAL QUESTIONS AND SCENARIOS FOR YOUR CONSIDERATION

Based on all we have discussed in this chapter, here are a few questions to encourage reflection and discussions with your own team;

1. **Cognitive Bias Awareness:**

    a. How aware are you of the various cognitive biases that can affect decision-making in GRC processes? Are there specific biases you or your organization have encountered?

    b. Can you think of a situation where a cognitive bias may have influenced a GRC decision or assessment? How did it impact the outcome?

    c. What steps can organizations take to foster a culture of bias awareness and mitigation among GRC professionals?

2. **Role of Technology:**

    a. In your organization, to what extent are AI, ML, and data-driven approaches currently used in GRC practices to mitigate cognitive biases? Are there areas where these technologies could be more effectively applied?

    b. How do you balance the need for human judgment with the objectivity of data-driven approaches in risk assessments and compliance efforts?

    c. What are the ethical considerations and potential challenges associated with the increased reliance on emerging technologies to mitigate cognitive biases?

3. **Legal and Financial Consequences:**

   a. How prepared is your organization to handle the legal and financial consequences of failing to account for biases in risk assessments? Do you have contingency plans in place?

   b. Have you encountered any examples of organizations that faced legal or financial repercussions due to biased risk assessments? What were the outcomes?

   c. How can organizations strike a balance between risk aversion and risk-taking in their GRC practices while minimizing the impact of biases?

4. **Regulatory and Compliance Frameworks:**

   a. How do regulatory bodies and compliance standards in your industry address the influence of cognitive biases on GRC practices? Are there areas where you see room for improvement in these frameworks?

   b. Can you identify any examples of organizations that have faced regulatory or legal challenges due to non-compliance resulting from cognitive biases in their GRC practices?

   c. How can organizations proactively align their GRC processes with regulatory and legal requirements while ensuring that bias mitigation is prioritized?

5. **Risk Mitigation and Ethical Behavior:**

   a. How can organizations strike a balance between risk mitigation and ethical behavior in their GRC practices? What ethical considerations should guide risk management decisions?

   b. Can you provide examples of organizations that have effectively integrated ethical standards and codes of conduct into their GRC processes? What were the outcomes?

c. How can GRC professionals promote a culture of ethical decision-making and objectivity in their organizations?

6. Future Challenges and Opportunities:

a. What do you see as the most significant challenges and opportunities in the GRC field as it relates to bias mitigation and decision-making in the coming years?

b. How might global events, technological advancements, or changes in regulations impact the way organizations approach GRC practices and bias mitigation?

c. What strategies can GRC professionals adopt to stay agile and responsive to evolving challenges in the GRC landscape?

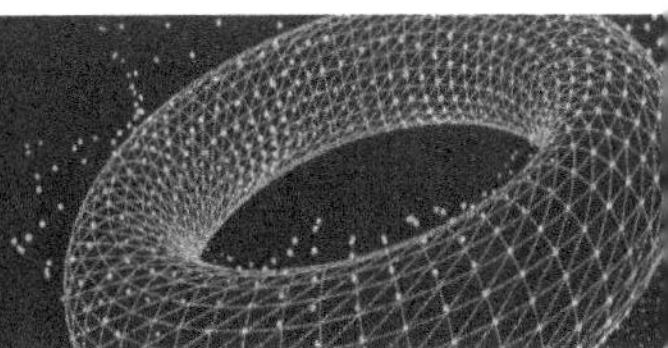

CHAPTER 3

THE PSYCHOLOGY OF COMPLIANCE: WHY DO PEOPLE ADHERE OR DEVIATE?

As the intricate web of governance, risk management, and compliance (GRC) continues to envelop the corporate landscape, one profound truth remains steadfast: at the heart of GRC lies the complicated and often enigmatic domain of human psychology. For in the grand design of rules, regulations, and mandates, it is the human element that brings life, nuance, and complexity to the practice of compliance.

In this chapter, we delve into the profound significance of understanding human psychology in the context of compliance, deciphering the intricate dance between the human mind and the intricate web of rules and regulations. Why do individuals adhere unwaveringly to compliance standards in some instances, while in others, they deviate with seemingly effortless disregard for the established norms? This is a question that has both confounded and captivated GRC experts, organizations, and scholars alike.

It is an aspect where the understanding of human nature becomes paramount, as the psychology of compliance unfolds as a fascinating tapestry of motivations, emotions, social influences, and cognitive processes. It transcends checkboxes and regulations, delving into the fundamental forces that guide human behavior within the framework of rules and standards.

The significance of understanding human psychology in compliance is undeniable. Compliance decisions are not driven solely by the written word of regulations; rather, they are the product of the complex interplay of individual and collective human minds. Without a profound understanding of the psychological underpinnings that govern these choices, organizations risk navigating the complex GRC landscape with a blindfold

THE ROLE OF COGNITIVE PROCESSES, MOTIVATION AND EMOTIONS IN COMPLIANCE

Most GRC experts will agree that the journey to unwavering adherence to rules and regulations is profoundly influenced by the intricate interplay of cognitive processes, motivations and emotions in the GRC field.

The understanding of these psychological elements is not a mere academic pursuit but a fundamental equipment for effective compliance and risk management.

COGNITIVE PROCESSES: THE FOUNDATION OF UNDERSTANDING

Cognition is the complex of mental processes and activities used in perceiving, remembering, and thinking and the act of using those processes (Cognitive Psychology, Pearsonhighered). The cognitive processes, of perception, memory, reasoning, and decision-making, serve as the foundation upon which compliance behaviors are built. Within the GRC landscape, cognitive processes play a pivotal role in how individuals and organizations interpret, retain, and apply complex regulatory information.

1. *Interpretation of Rules*: Cognitive processes shape how individuals and organizations interpret the multitude of rules and regulations that surround them. These processes influence whether one perceives a specific behavior as compliant or non-compliant, and how they integrate these interpretations into their daily activities.

2. *Learning from Experience*: Cognitive processes are responsible for retaining and learning from past experiences, both successful compliance and compliance failures. This memory and learning aspect of cognition is crucial for risk management and avoiding repeated compliance violations.

3. *Risk Assessment and Decision-Making:* Cognitive processes are deeply involved in assessing risks, making decisions, and evaluating the potential consequences of compliance or non-compliance. Clear thinking, analysis, and reasoning are essential when navigating complex GRC scenarios.

MOTIVATION: THE ENGINE OF COMPLIANCE

Motivation, the driving force that fuels our actions, plays a pivotal role in the realm of compliance. Motivation can be intrinsic or extrinsic, and understanding what motivates individuals and organizations to adhere to compliance standards is integral to effective GRC.

Intrinsic Motivation: This is the internal drive to adhere to compliance standards because it aligns with personal values or beliefs. GRC professionals often leverage intrinsic motivation by fostering a culture of ethics and integrity within an organization.

Extrinsic Motivation: External incentives, such as rewards or penalties, can influence compliance behavior. Compliance programs often use extrinsic motivation to encourage adherence through incentives, recognition, or consequences for non-compliance.

EMOTIONS: THE UNDERCURRENT OF DECISION-MAKING

Emotions, often the undercurrent of our decision-making processes, significantly impact compliance behaviors. Emotional responses can influence how individuals and organizations perceive compliance issues, approach risk, and make choices.

1. *Fear and Anxiety:* The fear of legal consequences, regulatory fines, or damage to reputation can strongly motivate compliance. Understanding these emotions can help organizations create effective deterrents.

2. *Ethical Emotions:* Emotions like guilt, shame, and pride can significantly impact compliance behaviors. Understanding the ethical dimensions of compliance can help foster a culture of moral responsibility.

3. *Trust and Confidence:* Positive emotions such as trust in leadership and confidence in the efficacy of compliance programs can encourage adherence. Building trust is a vital component of compliance success.

With a little digging, is it quite apparent how these cognitive processes, motivation, and emotions are not isolated elements but interconnected facets of the labyrinth called compliance. Organizations that acknowledge and integrate these psychological aspects into their GRC strategies can navigate the complex regulatory terrain with greater success.

FACTORS INFLUENCING ADHERENCE TO COMPLIANCE

The dynamics of human behavior, influenced by the social and peer context, play a noteworthy role in shaping adherence to compliance standards. Understanding the impact of social and peer pressure is crucial for GRC professionals seeking to foster a culture of compliance within organizations for long and short term benefits

SOCIAL NORMS AND CONFORMITY:

Social norms are unwritten rules and expectations that guide behavior within a group or society. In the context of compliance, social norms can strongly influence individuals' decisions to adhere to established rules and regulations. The desire to conform to these norms can exert a powerful force, leading individuals to align their behavior with what they perceive as socially accepted standards.

Peer Behavior: When individuals observe their peers adhering to compliance standards, they are more likely to follow suit. This is often referred to as the "bandwagon effect," where individuals align their behavior with that of their peers to avoid standing out or facing social disapproval.

Positive Role Models: Organizations can harness the power of positive role models within their workforce. When influential figures within an organization consistently demonstrate compliance behavior, it can inspire others to do the same.

SOCIAL PROOF AND VALIDATION:

Social pressure can also manifest in the form of social proof and validation. People tend to seek validation for their actions and decisions from their social circles. In the GRC context, this means that compliance decisions are often influenced by a desire for approval and validation from peers.

Reputation and Image: Maintaining a positive reputation and image within one's professional network is a strong motivator for adherence to compliance standards. Individuals are less likely to engage in non-compliant behavior if it risks tarnishing their professional standing.

Peer Review and Feedback: Peer reviews, feedback, and evaluations within an organization can serve as potent tools for shaping compliance behavior. Employees are motivated to receive positive feedback and validation from their peers and superiors.

ACCOUNTABILITY AND MORAL OBLIGATION:

Social and peer pressure can also create a sense of accountability and moral obligation. When individuals are aware that their actions are observed and evaluated by their peers, they are more likely to uphold compliance standards.

Collective Responsibility: Organizations can foster a sense of collective responsibility by emphasizing that compliance is not an individual endeavor but a shared commitment. When individuals perceive that their peers rely on them to uphold standards, they are more inclined to do so.

Whistleblower Programs: The presence of whistleblower programs and mechanisms for reporting non-compliance can be influenced by peer pressure. If individuals perceive that their peers are vigilant about reporting violations, it can create a deterrent effect on non-compliant behavior.

CHALLENGES OF SOCIAL AND PEER PRESSURE:

While social and peer pressure can be a powerful force for compliance, it also presents challenges. Peer pressure can sometimes lead to unethical behavior when a group collectively disregards compliance standards. This phenomenon, known as "groupthink," can lead to catastrophic consequences, and it's a risk that GRC professionals must be vigilant about.

The Impact of Ethical and Moral Considerations

The interplay between ethical principles, personal values and compliance regulations is a key contributor to individuals and organizations' view of compliance regulations. It guides them in embracing moral responsibility, making ethically sound compliance decisions and fostering an ethical culture that upholds the values of fairness, justice and greater social good.

Some of the major impact include;

1. **Ethical Frameworks in Compliance:**

    Ethical considerations provide the ethical framework upon which compliance decisions are often built. Ethical frameworks guide individuals and organizations in determining right from wrong, just from unjust, and fair from unfair. Within GRC, this ethical foundation is crucial for understanding the broader purpose and significance of compliance.

    Ethical Alignment: Ethical individuals and organizations are more likely to be aligned with compliance standards. When compliance aligns with deeply held ethical values, adherence becomes a natural extension of these values.

    Moral Integrity: Ethical and moral integrity often serve as a personal compass for individuals when making compliance decisions. Individuals who prioritize moral integrity are more likely to choose compliance even in challenging situations.

2. **Moral Responsibility and Duty:**

    Moral considerations frequently give rise to a sense of moral responsibility and duty to adhere to compliance standards. Moral responsibility implies that individuals and organizations view compliance as an obligation based on principles of fairness, justice, and societal good.

Moral Duty to Stakeholders: Organizations often perceive a moral duty to their stakeholders, including employees, customers, and the broader society, to adhere to compliance standards. This sense of duty is a powerful motivator for compliance.

Ethical Obligations in Decision-Making: Individuals making compliance decisions often weigh the ethical obligations that compliance carries. This can lead to decisions that prioritize the greater good over individual or organizational interests.

3. **Ethical Leadership and Organizational Culture:**

   Ethical leadership and the broader organizational culture can have a profound influence on adherence to compliance. Organizations with ethical leaders who set an example of moral conduct often see a ripple effect on compliance behavior.

   Tone from the Top: Ethical leaders set a tone from the top that emphasizes the importance of compliance as an ethical and moral imperative. This tone influences the entire organizational culture.

   Ethical Culture: An ethical organizational culture fosters an environment where compliance is not merely a legal requirement but a reflection of the organization's ethical principles. In such cultures, adherence to compliance is embedded in the organizational DNA.

4. **Ethical Dilemmas in Compliance:**

   The realm of GRC often presents complex ethical dilemmas, where compliance decisions may clash with other ethical considerations. For example, a compliance decision that avoids environmental harm but results in employee layoffs poses an ethical dilemma.

Balancing Ethical Principles: Individuals and organizations must navigate these dilemmas by balancing competing ethical principles. This requires a nuanced understanding of ethics and careful consideration of the consequences of compliance decisions.

5. **Consequences of Ethical Lapses:**

   Understanding the consequences of ethical lapses in compliance is also a key factor influencing adherence. Ethical lapses can lead to severe reputational damage, legal repercussions, and damage to stakeholder trust.

   Reputation and Trust: Ethical breaches in compliance can erode an organization's reputation and the trust of stakeholders. These consequences serve as a strong deterrent against non-compliance.

6. **Ethical Decision-Making Models:**

   The integration of ethical decision-making models, such as the ethical decision-making framework by Rest (1986), can provide guidance to individuals and organizations in making ethically sound compliance decisions. These models help navigate complex ethical considerations and apply them to compliance scenarios.

REAL-LIFE CASE STUDY OF SUCCESSFUL COMPLIANCE STRATEGIES AND INSTANCES OF NON-COMPLIANCE

These real-world examples showcase the importance of robust compliance strategies and the severe consequences of non-compliance. Successful compliance involves a commitment to ethical conduct, transparency, proactive risk management, and a culture that prioritizes adherence to regulatory standards. In contrast, instances of non-compliance often result from ethical lapses, governance failures, and a disregard for legal and regulatory requirements. Organizations can learn valuable lessons from these cases to strengthen their own GRC frameworks and promote a culture of integrity and compliance.

SUCCESSFUL COMPLIANCE STRATEGIES:

MICROSOFT'S COMPLIANCE FRAMEWORK:

Microsoft has implemented a robust compliance framework that aligns with various regulatory requirements and industry standards.

Key Strategies:

Integration of Compliance into Product Development: Microsoft incorporates compliance considerations into the design and development of its products, ensuring security and privacy by design.

Regular Audits and Assessments: The company conducts regular internal audits and assessments to monitor compliance with data protection regulations and other industry standards.

Global Data Protection Commitment: Microsoft's commitment to global data protection standards, such as GDPR, demonstrates a proactive approach to compliance on a global scale.

JOHNSON & JOHNSON'S CREDO:

Johnson & Johnson has a long-standing commitment to its "Credo," a set of values that guide the company's decisions and actions.

Key Strategies:

Ethical Leadership: The company places a strong emphasis on ethical leadership, fostering a culture where compliance is embedded in decision-making at all levels.

Compliance Education and Training: Johnson & Johnson invests in comprehensive compliance education and training programs to ensure employees understand and adhere to ethical standards.

External Collaborations: The company collaborates with external organizations and regulatory bodies to stay updated on compliance requirements and industry best practices.

INSTANCES OF NON-COMPLIANCE:

ENRON SCANDAL:

Background: Enron's financial scandal in the early 2000s is one of the most infamous cases of corporate non-compliance.

Key Non-Compliance Factors:

Accounting Irregularities: Enron engaged in deceptive accounting practices to inflate its financial statements, providing a misleading picture of the company's financial health.

Lack of Transparency: The company failed to maintain transparency regarding its financial dealings, hiding debt in off-balance-sheet entities.

Corporate Governance Failures: Enron's board and management were implicated in a lack of oversight, contributing to a culture that prioritized short-term financial gains over ethical conduct.

VOLKSWAGEN'S EMISSIONS SCANDAL:

Background: Volkswagen (VW) faced a major scandal in 2015 when it was revealed that the company had installed software to cheat emissions tests in its diesel vehicles.

Key Non-Compliance Factors:

Emission Test Manipulation: VW intentionally manipulated emission tests to meet regulatory standards, deceiving both regulators and consumers.

Lack of Ethical Oversight: The scandal highlighted a lack of ethical oversight within the company, with top executives allegedly involved in the decision to deploy the deceptive software.

Reputational Damage: The non-compliance significantly damaged VW's reputation, leading to legal consequences, fines, and a decline in market trust.

Building A Compliance-Focused Culture

There are many possible approaches that can be taken towards building a compliance-focused culture in an organization. To achieve a sustainable framework should be the aim in order to ensure long-term benefits even as new employees come in and old ones leave. A few key steps have been listed below:

Leadership Commitment:

Lead by Example: Executives and leaders should exemplify a strong commitment to compliance through their actions and decisions. When leadership demonstrates ethical behavior, it sets a powerful precedent for the entire organization.

Communicate Expectations: Clearly communicate the importance of compliance and ethical conduct. Leaders should articulate their expectations regarding adherence to regulatory requirements and ethical standards.

Integration into Organizational Values:

Incorporate into Mission and Vision Statements: Integrate compliance into the organization's mission and vision statements. Clearly express the commitment to ethical behavior and regulatory compliance as core values driving the organization's purpose.

Performance Metrics: Include compliance metrics in performance evaluations. Aligning individual and team performance with compliance goals reinforces the importance of adherence to ethical and regulatory standards.

COLLABORATION WITH STAKEHOLDERS:

Engage External Stakeholders: Collaborate with external stakeholders, including regulatory bodies and industry peers, to stay informed about evolving compliance requirements and best practices. External engagement contributes to a holistic approach to compliance.

Industry Benchmarking: Benchmark the organization's compliance practices against industry standards. This benchmarking process can identify areas for improvement and ensure that the organization remains at the forefront of compliance within its sector.

TECHNOLOGICAL INTEGRATION:

Use of GRC Software: Implement Governance, Risk, and Compliance (GRC) software to streamline compliance processes, track metrics, and manage risk effectively. Technology can enhance the efficiency and effectiveness of compliance initiatives.

Data Analytics for Monitoring: Utilize data analytics tools to monitor compliance metrics and detect potential issues. Data-driven insights contribute to proactive risk management and compliance oversight.

FUTURE TRENDS IN COMPLIANCE PSYCHOLOGY

For those who intend to stay ahead of the curve, developing more robust and adaptive compliance strategies that resonate with the complexities of human behavior is a must. It's crucial to anticipate and discuss emerging trends in compliance psychology so as to keep with the latest facts and opportunities. Here are some anticipated trends:

1. **Behavioral Science Integration:**

   Incorporation into Compliance Programs: There will be an increased integration of behavioral science principles into compliance programs. Organizations will leverage insights from psychology to design more effective training, communication, and incentive structures that align with how individuals make decisions.

   Nudging Techniques: The application of "nudging" techniques, derived from behavioral economics, will become more prevalent. Nudges aim to influence behavior in a predictable way without restricting options, aligning with a softer approach to encourage compliance.

2. **Technology and Data Analytics:**

   Predictive Analytics for Non-Compliance: The use of predictive analytics and machine learning in compliance programs will rise. Organizations will employ these technologies to identify patterns and predict potential areas of non-compliance, allowing for proactive interventions.

   Personalized Compliance Solutions: Technology will enable the development of personalized compliance solutions. Customized training modules, communication strategies, and incentives based on individual psychological profiles will become more common.

3. **Ethical Decision-Making Models:**

   Development of Ethical Decision-Making Models: Organizations will focus on developing and implementing ethical decision-making models. These models will guide employees through ethical dilemmas, incorporating psychological principles to enhance moral reasoning and judgment.

   Integration with AI Ethics: As artificial intelligence (AI) becomes more prevalent, there will be a growing emphasis on integrating ethical decision-making models into AI systems. This ensures that automated processes align with human values and ethical considerations.

4. **Gamification and Engagement:**

Gamification for Training: Gamification principles will be increasingly employed in compliance training programs. Incorporating game-like elements, such as challenges, rewards, and interactive scenarios, can enhance engagement and knowledge retention.

Virtual Reality (VR) for Compliance Simulations: The use of virtual reality for compliance simulations will gain traction. VR technology provides immersive and realistic scenarios, allowing individuals to practice decision-making in compliance-related situations.

5. **Cultural and Inclusive Approaches:**

Cultural Sensitivity in Compliance Programs: Compliance psychology will place a stronger emphasis on cultural sensitivity. Organizations will tailor compliance programs to the cultural nuances of diverse workforces, recognizing that one-size-fits-all approaches may not be effective.

Inclusive Language and Communication: There will be a shift towards more inclusive language and communication strategies in compliance materials. Acknowledging diverse perspectives and experiences fosters a sense of belonging and increases the effectiveness of compliance messaging.

6. **Neuroethics and Brain Science:**

Exploration of Neuroethics: The exploration of neuroethics, examining the ethical implications of neuroscience advancements, will become more prevalent. Organizations may delve into the ethical considerations of using neuroscientific insights in compliance strategies.

Understanding Cognitive Biases: A deeper understanding of cognitive biases through advancements in brain science will inform compliance approaches. Strategies to mitigate biases and enhance decision-making will be refined based on neuroscientific research.

7. **Continuous Monitoring and Adaptive Learning:**

Continuous Monitoring of Psychological Factors: Organizations will move towards continuous monitoring of psychological factors influencing compliance. This involves regularly assessing the psychological climate within the organization and adjusting strategies accordingly.

Adaptive Learning Platforms: Compliance training platforms will adopt adaptive learning techniques. These platforms will dynamically adjust content based on individual progress, learning preferences, and psychological profiles, optimizing the effectiveness of training.

8. **Regulatory Technology (RegTech):**

RegTech Solutions for Behavioral Analysis: RegTech solutions will increasingly incorporate behavioral analysis capabilities. These tools can analyze user behavior to detect anomalies, identify potential areas of non-compliance, and provide insights for risk management.

Blockchain for Transparency and Trust: The use of blockchain technology will contribute to transparency and trust in compliance processes. Blockchain's decentralized and tamper-resistant nature can enhance the integrity of compliance-related data.

9. Cross-Disciplinary Collaboration:

Collaboration with Psychology Experts: Organizations will foster cross-disciplinary collaboration, bringing in experts from psychology and related fields to inform compliance strategies. This collaboration will enhance the depth and effectiveness of compliance programs.

Integration with Organizational Psychology: The integration of organizational psychology principles will become more prominent. Understanding group dynamics, leadership impact, and employee motivations from an organizational psychology perspective will inform compliance culture initiatives.

CHAPTER 4

EMPATHY IN GRC: UNDERSTANDING STAKEHOLDER CONCERNS AND NEEDS.

Empathy, the ability to understand and share the feelings of others, emerges as a transformative force within the GRC landscape. It transcends mere procedural compliance, inviting GRC professionals to don the empathetic lens, revealing a nuanced understanding of stakeholder concerns and needs. In this chapter, we embark on a journey to unravel the layers of empathy in GRC, exploring its significance, applications, and the profound impact it can have on the success of GRC endeavors.

Stakeholders, with their diverse concerns, needs, and aspirations, are the beating heart of any GRC ecosystem. Amidst the labyrinth of regulations and risk assessments, empathy emerges as the unsung hero, the magical thread that weaves strong and enduring relationships with stakeholders.

When GRC professionals demonstrate empathy, they signal to stakeholders that their concerns are not just entries on a compliance checklist but vital components of a shared narrative. This understanding fosters a connection that goes beyond the formalities of governance. Stakeholders feel seen, heard, and valued—an essential foundation for any robust and enduring relationship.

BEYOND COMPLIANCE: ADDRESSING EMOTIONAL NEEDS

Stakeholders, like any human beings, have emotional needs intertwined with their professional concerns. Empathy allows GRC professionals to address not only the regulatory requirements but also the emotional landscape of compliance. It is the tool that turns a regulatory update into a shared dialogue, a policy change into a collaborative effort, and a risk assessment into a joint exploration of potential challenges and solutions.

Understanding stakeholders on this emotional level creates an environment where not only compliance goals are achieved but where individuals feel supported and heard throughout the process. It transforms GRC from a set of imposed rules to a shared commitment to success.

NAVIGATING CHALLENGES WITH EMPATHETIC SOLUTIONS

Regulatory changes, unforeseen risks, and organizational shifts can create a tumultuous sea to navigate. Empathy, however, becomes the compass that guides GRC professionals through these storms. By understanding the unique challenges faced by stakeholders, solutions can be tailored to address not just the immediate issues but also the underlying concerns.

Empathetic problem-solving is not just about finding solutions; it's about crafting solutions that resonate with the stakeholders on a personal level. It transforms challenges into opportunities for strengthened relationships and shared growth.

EMPATHY UNVEILED: A CATALYST FOR EFFECTIVE GOVERNANCE AND RISK MANAGEMENT

Far from being a soft skill confined to interpersonal interactions, empathy emerges as a dynamic catalyst that propels effective governance and risk management into realms previously unexplored.

1. **Understanding the Stakeholder Landscape**

    At the heart of effective governance lies a deep understanding of the stakeholders who navigate the GRC landscape. Empathy becomes the lens through which GRC professionals perceive and comprehend the intricacies of stakeholder concerns. It goes beyond the surface, unraveling the layers of motivations, fears, and aspirations that shape the stakeholder landscape.

    This understanding becomes a strategic advantage in governance, allowing for the formulation of policies and practices that not only comply with regulations but resonate with the diverse needs of those they govern. Empathy becomes the compass that guides governance decisions, ensuring they align with the ever-evolving expectations of stakeholders.

2. **Anticipating and Mitigating Risks Through Empathetic Insights**

    Risk management, a terrain fraught with uncertainties and potential pitfalls, gains a valuable ally in empathy. By immersing themselves in the perspectives of stakeholders, GRC professionals become adept at anticipating risks before they manifest. Empathy unveils the nuanced aspects of stakeholder behavior, providing insights into potential deviations and challenges that may arise.

    Empathetic risk management goes beyond statistical models and quantitative assessments; it delves into the realm of qualitative understanding. GRC professionals, armed with empathetic insights, can craft risk mitigation strategies that not only address the tangible risks but also factor in the emotional and cultural dimensions that may influence risk outcomes.

3. **Building a Culture of Compliance Through Connection**

Compliance, often perceived as a set of rules and procedures, takes on a new dimension when viewed through the concept of empathy. Empathy becomes the bridge that connects GRC professionals and stakeholders in a shared commitment to compliance. It transforms compliance from a set of imposed regulations to a collaborative effort where both parties actively contribute to the culture of adherence.

A culture of compliance nurtured by empathy is not solely about avoiding penalties; it becomes a shared ethos that aligns with the values and expectations of stakeholders. GRC professionals, by understanding the emotional and practical implications of compliance measures, can craft policies that are not just followed but embraced.

4. **Enhancing Communication and Transparency:**

Effective governance and risk management hinge on clear and transparent communication. Empathy becomes the key to unlocking impactful communication channels. By understanding the concerns and communication preferences of stakeholders, GRC professionals can tailor messages that resonate.

Empathy also fosters transparency by acknowledging when things go awry. GRC professionals, guided by empathy, are more likely to communicate openly about challenges and setbacks. This transparent communication not only builds trust but also allows for collaborative problem-solving, preventing minor issues from escalating into major risks.

EMPATHY AS A CORE COMPETENCY IN GRC: NAVIGATING THE HUMAN DIMENSION

Empathy is considered a new skill that transcends the realms of technical expertise and procedural acumen. It is an indispensable skill that positions GRC professionals not only as guardians of compliance but as navigators of the intricate human dimension inherent in every GRC endeavor.

1. **Beyond Technical Expertise:**

    While technical expertise remains fundamental in GRC, the inclusion of empathy as a core competency expands the professional toolkit. GRC professionals are not merely interpreters of regulations and architects of risk management frameworks; they are interpreters of human needs, concerns, and aspirations. Empathy elevates their role from enforcers to collaborators, fostering a synergy between regulatory requirements and the human experience.

2. **Understanding Stakeholder Perspectives:**

    The essence of GRC lies in the relationships between the governing and the governed. Empathy allows GRC professionals to navigate this intricate web by understanding the diverse perspectives of stakeholders. It is the bridge that connects compliance measures to the human impact they entail. By acknowledging and comprehending the concerns and expectations of stakeholders, GRC professionals become adept at aligning GRC practices with the lived experiences of those they serve.

3. **Effective Communication and Collaboration:**

    Effective communication is the lifeblood of meaningful relationships. In the world today, empathy has become the language that resonates with stakeholders. GRC professionals, equipped with empathetic communication skills, can convey complex regulatory requirements in a manner that is not just understandable but relatable. This fosters a collaborative environment where stakeholders actively engage in the compliance journey, transforming GRC from a top-down imposition to a shared commitment.

4. **Navigating Cultural Sensitivities:**

The globalized nature of business demands an acute awareness of cultural nuances. Empathy allows GRC professionals to navigate the intricacies of cultural sensitivities, ensuring that compliance practices are not one-size-fits-all. By recognizing and respecting cultural diversities, GRC professionals can tailor strategies that resonate with the unique values and norms of different stakeholders, fostering a more inclusive and harmonious GRC environment.

5. **Building Trust Through Emotional Intelligence:**

Trust is the bedrock of successful GRC endeavors. Empathy, intertwined with emotional intelligence, becomes the cornerstone of trust-building. GRC professionals who possess the ability to understand and respond to the emotional needs of stakeholders create an atmosphere of trust. Stakeholders are more likely to trust those who not only comprehend the technical aspects of compliance but also demonstrate an understanding of the human impact of GRC decisions.

6. **Anticipating and Mitigating Resistance:**

Change, inherent in the GRC landscape, often meets resistance. Empathy equips GRC professionals with the ability to anticipate and address resistance by understanding the fears, uncertainties, and concerns of stakeholders. Rather than viewing resistance as a hurdle, GRC professionals with empathetic competencies see it as an opportunity for dialogue and collaboration, paving the way for smoother transitions in compliance measures.

7. **Strengthening Organizational Culture:**

   Organizational culture is a reflection of shared values and behaviors. Empathy, when embedded as a core competency, becomes a catalyst for a culture of compliance and ethical behavior. GRC professionals, by leading with empathy, inspire a culture where ethical considerations are not just compliance checkboxes but guiding principles that permeate every aspect of organizational conduct.

STRATEGIES FOR ACTIVELY IDENTIFYING AND RECOGNIZING STAKEHOLDER CONCERNS IN GRC

To proactively address stakeholder needs, GRC professionals can employ strategic approaches to identify and recognize their concerns long before they become stumbling blocks to the process of building a culture of compliance within any organization:

1. **Stakeholder Surveys and Feedback Mechanisms:**

   Implementing regular surveys and feedback mechanisms is a direct and efficient way to gather insights into stakeholder concerns. Design surveys that encompass various aspects of the GRC process, including compliance measures, risk management strategies, and communication effectiveness. Encourage stakeholders to provide open-ended feedback, allowing them to articulate their concerns in their own words.

2. **Stakeholder Workshops and Focus Groups:**

   Organize stakeholder workshops and focus groups to create a collaborative environment for open discussions. These interactive sessions provide a platform for stakeholders to voice their concerns, share perspectives, and engage in constructive dialogue. Workshops and focus groups can unveil nuanced concerns that might not surface in traditional surveys.

3. Continuous Stakeholder Engagement:

Establish a culture of continuous stakeholder engagement, where communication is not limited to specific milestones or compliance deadlines. Regularly communicate updates, changes, and relevant information, and create channels for stakeholders to express their concerns in real-time. This ongoing engagement fosters a sense of transparency and accessibility.

4. Data Analytics and Trend Analysis:

Leverage data analytics and trend analysis tools to scrutinize patterns and identify potential concerns. Analyzing data related to compliance metrics, risk incidents, and stakeholder interactions can reveal emerging trends that may indicate underlying concerns. This data-driven approach allows GRC professionals to stay ahead of potential issues.

5. Social Listening and Online Presence Monitoring:

In the digital age, stakeholders often express concerns through various online channels. Implement social listening tools to monitor online conversations, forums, and social media platforms for discussions related to GRC practices. This proactive approach enables GRC professionals to identify and respond to concerns expressed in the digital realm.

6. One-on-One Stakeholder Interviews:

Conduct one-on-one interviews with key stakeholders to delve deeper into their concerns and expectations. These personalized conversations provide a more intimate understanding of individual perspectives. Use these interviews to uncover specific pain points, gather qualitative insights, and build stronger relationships with key stakeholders.

7. **Cross-Functional Collaboration:**

   Collaborate with other departments and teams within the organization to gain a holistic view of stakeholder concerns. Cross-functional collaboration ensures that concerns related to GRC are not siloed but are integrated into the broader organizational context. Engage with departments such as customer service, legal, and operations to gather comprehensive insights.

8. **Scenario Planning and Risk Workshops:**

   Conduct scenario planning and risk workshops that involve stakeholders in discussions about potential future challenges. Through interactive exercises, stakeholders can express their concerns about hypothetical scenarios, allowing GRC professionals to anticipate and address potential risks before they materialize.

9. **Regulatory Change Impact Assessments:**

   Stay proactive in monitoring and assessing the impact of regulatory changes on stakeholders. Implement a systematic process for evaluating how new regulations may affect different stakeholder groups. By anticipating the implications of regulatory changes, GRC professionals can address concerns and communicate effectively with stakeholders.

10. **Key Performance Indicators (KPIs) for Stakeholder Satisfaction:**

    Establish KPIs related to stakeholder satisfaction and regularly assess these metrics. Track trends over time and set benchmarks for acceptable levels of satisfaction. KPIs provide measurable indicators of stakeholder contentment and help identify areas that require attention.

Empathy in Risk Communication: Bridging the Gap Between Data and Emotion

Effectively communicating risks to stakeholders is a delicate art, requiring a nuanced understanding of not just the data but the human emotions intertwined with the information. Empathy emerges as a crucial element in this communication process, acting as the bridge that connects the technical aspects of risk with the emotional responses of stakeholders.

1. **Understanding Stakeholder Perspectives:**

   Empathy begins with a genuine effort to understand the diverse perspectives of stakeholders. Different individuals and groups may perceive risks differently based on their roles, experiences, and values. By empathetically acknowledging these diverse perspectives, risk communicators can tailor their messages to resonate with the unique concerns and expectations of various stakeholders.

2. **Acknowledging Emotional Responses:**

   Risk communication often evokes emotional responses, ranging from anxiety and fear to curiosity and confusion. Empathy involves acknowledging and validating these emotional reactions. Instead of dismissing emotions, empathetic communication recognizes them as valid components of the stakeholder experience. This acknowledgment builds trust by demonstrating that the communicator understands the human impact of the communicated risks.

3. **Clear and Transparent Messaging:**

   Empathy emphasizes the importance of clear, transparent, and accessible messaging. Risk communicators need to convey complex information in a manner that is easily understood by stakeholders with varying levels of expertise. Empathetic communication avoids jargon and technical language, opting for plain language that resonates with the intended audience. Clarity and transparency enhance stakeholder comprehension and mitigate the potential for misinformation or misunderstanding.

4. **Tailoring Communication Styles:**

   Different stakeholders may have distinct communication preferences and styles. Empathy involves adapting the communication approach to align with the preferences of the audience. Some stakeholders may prefer detailed reports, while others may respond better to visual presentations or interactive discussions. By tailoring communication styles, risk communicators demonstrate an understanding of the diverse ways in which stakeholders absorb and process information.

5. **Anticipating and Addressing Concerns:**

   Empathy equips risk communicators with the ability to anticipate and address stakeholder concerns before they escalate. By placing themselves in the shoes of stakeholders, communicators can proactively identify potential worries and uncertainties. Addressing these concerns in advance fosters a sense of reassurance and demonstrates a commitment to stakeholder well-being.

6. **Humanizing Data with Real-World Examples:**

   Empathetic risk communication goes beyond presenting statistical data; it humanizes risks with real-world examples and relatable scenarios. By illustrating the potential impact of risks on individuals, communities, or the organization itself, risk communicators make the information more tangible and emotionally resonant. Real-world examples evoke empathy by connecting stakeholders to the human stories behind the data.

7. **Two-Way Communication and Feedback:**

Empathy encourages a two-way communication approach that invites stakeholders to express their thoughts, concerns, and questions. Actively seeking and listening to stakeholder feedback creates a dialogue rather than a monologue. This open communication channel allows risk communicators to address evolving concerns and adapt their messaging based on the real-time needs of stakeholders.

8. **Empathetic Tone and Demeanor:**

The tone and demeanor of risk communicators play a significant role in conveying empathy. A compassionate and empathetic tone communicates genuine concern for stakeholders' well-being. It involves expressing empathy not only through words but also through non-verbal cues, such as body language and tone of voice.

9. **Providing Actionable Guidance:**

Empathetic risk communication includes providing actionable guidance for stakeholders. Rather than leaving individuals feeling overwhelmed by the presented risks, communicators offer practical steps and guidance on how stakeholders can mitigate or manage these risks. This proactive approach empowers stakeholders to take informed actions, contributing to a sense of control and security.

10. **Continuous Engagement and Support:**

Empathy extends beyond isolated communication moments; it involves continuous engagement and support. Risk communicators actively check in with stakeholders, providing updates, addressing emerging concerns, and offering ongoing support. This sustained engagement reinforces the empathetic approach and builds a foundation of trust over time.

NAVIGATING DIVERSITY IN STAKEHOLDER PERSPECTIVES: A CALL FOR UNDERSTANDING AND ADAPTATION

In GRC, managing stakeholder idiosyncrasies, effectively communicating with them alongside the many other responsibilities of safeguarding systems and data is akin to a balancing act. To effectively navigate this complex terrain, experts in GRC must recognize the imperative of understanding and adapting to diverse stakeholder perspectives.

1. **The Mosaic of Perspectives:**

   Stakeholders are not homogenous entities; they are individuals with diverse backgrounds, experiences, and perspectives. Understanding this diversity is not merely a courtesy; it is an essential prerequisite for effective GRC. Each stakeholder, whether internal or external, brings a distinctive lens through which they view and interpret GRC initiatives. Recognizing and appreciating this mosaic of perspectives is foundational to building meaningful connections.

2. **Cultural Sensitivity:**

   In an interconnected global landscape, organizations often operate across cultural boundaries. Cultural nuances significantly influence how stakeholders perceive and engage with GRC practices. Empathy involves not only recognizing cultural differences but also being sensitive to them. GRC professionals must adapt their approaches to align with diverse cultural norms, values, and communication styles, fostering an environment of inclusivity.

3. **Tailoring Communication Strategies:**

   Communication is the bridge that connects GRC professionals with stakeholders. Understanding diverse perspectives requires tailoring communication strategies to resonate with different audiences. Some stakeholders may prefer detailed reports, while others may respond better to visual presentations or interactive discussions. Adapting communication styles demonstrates a commitment to meeting stakeholders where they are, facilitating clearer understanding.

4. Industry-Specific Considerations:

Industries vary in their operations, risks, and compliance requirements. Stakeholders from different industries may prioritize distinct aspects of GRC based on their sector-specific challenges and expectations. GRC professionals need to delve into the intricacies of each industry, understanding the unique concerns and adapting GRC strategies accordingly. Industry-specific nuances should be woven into the fabric of GRC practices.

5. Internal vs. External Stakeholder Dynamics:

Internal and external stakeholders often have divergent perspectives on GRC initiatives. While internal stakeholders may focus on operational efficiency and internal controls, external stakeholders may prioritize transparency and ethical conduct. Recognizing these inherent differences allows GRC professionals to tailor their strategies to address the specific expectations and concerns of each group.

6. Legal and Regulatory Variances:

Legal and regulatory landscapes vary across jurisdictions, adding another layer of complexity to stakeholder perspectives. GRC professionals must navigate these variances by understanding the intricacies of local laws and regulations. Adapting GRC practices to comply with jurisdiction-specific requirements demonstrates a commitment to ethical conduct and legal compliance, fostering trust among stakeholders.

7. **Varying Risk Appetites:**

   Stakeholders possess different risk appetites influenced by their roles, experiences, and organizational objectives. Understanding and adapting to varying risk appetites is crucial for aligning GRC strategies with stakeholders' comfort levels. Some stakeholders may be risk-averse, while others may be more inclined to embrace calculated risks. GRC professionals must tailor risk management approaches to accommodate this spectrum of risk tolerances.

8. **Stakeholder Lifecycle Dynamics:**

   Stakeholder perspectives evolve throughout their engagement with an organization. A customer may have different concerns compared to an investor or a long-term employee. GRC professionals should recognize the lifecycle dynamics of stakeholders and adapt their strategies accordingly. Early engagement may require educational approaches, while long-term stakeholders may benefit from more nuanced, relationship-focused initiatives.

9. **Social Responsibility and Ethical Considerations:**

   Diverse stakeholder perspectives often encompass social responsibility and ethical considerations. GRC professionals must grasp the ethical expectations of stakeholders and adapt GRC practices to align with broader societal values. Recognizing the interconnectedness of GRC with social responsibility fosters a positive reputation and trust among stakeholders who prioritize ethical conduct.

10. **Adapting to Evolving Perspectives:**

    Perspectives are not static; they evolve over time based on experiences, industry trends, and global shifts. GRC professionals must remain agile in adapting their approaches to accommodate evolving stakeholder perspectives. Regularly reassessing and recalibrating GRC strategies ensures alignment with the dynamic expectations of stakeholders.

Navigating Challenges in Integrating Empathy into GRC Practices

While the integration of empathy into Governance, Risk Management, and Compliance (GRC) practices holds immense potential, it is not without its challenges. Recognizing and addressing these challenges is crucial for cultivating a GRC framework that authentically embraces empathy. Here are common hurdles and strategies for navigating them:

1. **Balancing Compliance and Empathy:**

   Challenge: GRC inherently revolves around compliance with regulations and risk management, which may be perceived as conflicting with the empathetic consideration of stakeholder needs.

   Strategy: Establish a symbiotic relationship between compliance and empathy by framing compliance measures in the context of stakeholder well-being. Emphasize that ethical conduct and understanding stakeholder perspectives enhance, rather than compromise, compliance efforts.

2. **Data Privacy and Confidentiality Concerns:**

   Challenge: GRC often involves handling sensitive information, raising concerns about maintaining data privacy and confidentiality while practicing empathy.

   Strategy: Implement robust data protection measures and clearly communicate the boundaries of confidentiality to stakeholders. Highlight the organization's commitment to ethical information handling while ensuring that empathetic practices remain within legal and ethical boundaries.

3. **Resistance to Change:**

Challenge: Introducing empathy as a core competency may face resistance from individuals accustomed to traditional, more rigid GRC approaches.

Strategy: Foster a culture of openness to change by highlighting the benefits of empathy in enhancing collaboration, stakeholder relationships, and overall GRC effectiveness. Provide training and support to facilitate the transition and demonstrate the positive impact of empathy on organizational outcomes.

4. **Measuring and Quantifying Empathy:**

Challenge: Empathy is inherently subjective and challenging to measure, making it difficult to quantify its impact on GRC practices.

Strategy: Adopt a multifaceted approach to assessment, combining quantitative metrics (such as stakeholder satisfaction scores) with qualitative insights (gathered through interviews and case studies). Acknowledge the subjective nature of empathy while leveraging measurable indicators linked to positive outcomes.

5. **Cultural and Diversity Sensitivity:**

Challenge: GRC initiatives often span diverse cultural and organizational contexts, requiring an understanding of unique perspectives and potential challenges.

Strategy: Prioritize cultural competence in GRC professionals through training programs that emphasize diversity sensitivity. Establish communication channels for stakeholders to express cultural concerns and adapt GRC strategies to accommodate diverse perspectives.

6. **Time Constraints in Decision-Making:**

Challenge: GRC decisions often need to be made promptly, leaving limited time for thorough empathetic considerations.

Strategy: Embed empathetic decision-making principles into GRC processes to streamline the integration of empathy. Provide decision-makers with tools and frameworks that allow for a rapid yet empathetic assessment of stakeholder perspectives.

7. **Ensuring Consistency Across Teams:**

Challenge: Achieving consistency in empathetic practices across different GRC teams or departments may pose a challenge.

Strategy: Standardize empathetic practices by establishing clear guidelines and protocols. Foster a culture of knowledge-sharing and collaboration to ensure that successful empathetic approaches are disseminated and adopted consistently across the organization.

8. **Resistance from Traditional GRC Structures:**

Challenge: Traditional GRC structures may resist the integration of empathy, viewing it as a deviation from established protocols.

Strategy: Foster a gradual shift by emphasizing the complementary nature of empathy to existing GRC practices. Showcase success stories where empathetic considerations have led to positive outcomes, gradually building a case for the integration of empathy into traditional structures.

9. **Navigating Conflicting Stakeholder Interests:**

    Challenge: Stakeholders may have conflicting interests, making it challenging to balance and address diverse perspectives empathetically.

    Strategy: Prioritize transparency in communicating decisions and engage stakeholders in a collaborative dialogue. Clearly articulate the rationale behind decisions, acknowledging conflicting interests and demonstrating a commitment to fair and inclusive decision-making.

10. **Maintaining Professional Boundaries:**

    Challenge: GRC professionals may struggle to maintain a balance between empathy and maintaining professional boundaries, risking potential bias or compromise.

    Strategy: Provide training on ethical considerations and maintaining professional boundaries while practicing empathy. Establish clear guidelines on when and how empathy should be applied to ensure consistency and avoid potential pitfalls.

REAL-WORLD EXAMPLES OF SUCCESSFUL APPLICATIONS OF EMPATHY IN GRC

1. **Wells Fargo's Ethical Rebuilding:**

    In the aftermath of the Wells Fargo account scandal, the bank faced a severe trust deficit with customers and stakeholders.

    Empathy in Action: Wells Fargo initiated an empathetic response by acknowledging the wrongdoing, apologizing to affected customers, and committing to ethical rebuilding. They established transparency in communication, conducted customer outreach programs, and implemented changes to prevent similar issues in the future. The empathetic approach helped rebuild trust and demonstrated a commitment to stakeholder well-being.

2. Microsoft's Accessibility Initiatives:

Ensuring that technology is accessible to all users, including those with disabilities, is a growing concern for organizations like Microsoft.

Empathy in Action: Microsoft has integrated empathy into its GRC practices by prioritizing accessibility in product design and compliance initiatives. Their commitment to inclusive design is exemplified through features like "Seeing AI" and accessible design guidelines. By considering the diverse needs of users, Microsoft not only complies with accessibility standards but also enhances the overall user experience.

3. Johnson & Johnson's Crisis Response:

During the Tylenol crisis in the 1980s, Johnson & Johnson faced the urgent need to address public safety concerns and protect its reputation.

Empathy in Action: Johnson & Johnson demonstrated empathy by prioritizing public safety over profits. They immediately recalled Tylenol products, communicated transparently with the public, and introduced tamper-resistant packaging. This empathetic crisis response not only adhered to regulatory requirements but also showcased a deep commitment to stakeholder well-being, ultimately preserving the company's reputation.

4. **Salesforce's Stakeholder Engagement:**

As a global leader in cloud-based services, Salesforce faces the challenge of addressing the diverse needs and concerns of a wide range of stakeholders.

Empathy in Action: Salesforce incorporates empathy into its GRC practices by actively engaging with stakeholders through various channels. The company regularly seeks feedback, conducts surveys, and holds community events to understand the unique perspectives of its diverse user base. This empathetic approach enhances stakeholder relationships, contributing to a more comprehensive and inclusive GRC strategy.

5. **Airbnb's Anti-Discrimination Initiatives:**

Airbnb encountered issues related to discrimination, with reports of hosts discriminating against guests based on race or other factors.

Empathy in Action: Airbnb responded empathetically by acknowledging the problem and implementing anti-discrimination measures. They introduced features like Instant Book, which allows guests to book without host approval, reducing the potential for biased decision-making. Airbnb also launched initiatives to promote diversity and inclusion within its host community, addressing the root causes of discrimination and enhancing its GRC framework.

CHAPTER 5

Human-Centric Design: Creating User-Friendly Security Policies

User-friendly policies act as a cohesive force, ensuring that security measures are not only comprehensive but also comprehensible to those who must navigate them daily. This approach transforms compliance from a burdensome obligation into a shared responsibility, empowering individuals

Beyond mere regulatory checkboxes, these policies serve as the conduit between the intricate web of governance frameworks and the individuals tasked with implementation. In practice, security policies are written in natural language in a document and must then be deployed either in an organizational or in a technical manner (Rudolf 2015). By fostering clarity and comprehension, user-friendly policies not only fortify an organization's defenses but also cultivate a culture of awareness and adherence.

Moreover, in an era where digital transformation is ubiquitous, user-friendly security policies become instrumental in bridging the gap between technological advancements and human adaptability. As organizations strive for agility and innovation, policies that are approachable and easily understood become catalysts for seamless integration of security measures into everyday workflows.

THE CHALLENGES OF TRADITIONAL COMPLEX POLICIES

Firstly, the complex nature of these policies often results in a lack of clarity, making it arduous for individuals at all levels of an organization to comprehend and implement them effectively. This opacity not only hampers understanding but also increases the likelihood of unintentional non-compliance.

Furthermore, the intricate language and technical jargon embedded in complex policies create a substantial barrier to entry for individuals without a deep understanding of cybersecurity nuances. This linguistic challenge not only alienates non-specialists but also inhibits effective communication between different stakeholders, hindering the collaborative effort required for robust GRC.

Traditional policies, characterized by their rigidity, struggle to adapt to the dynamic landscape of cyber threats. As new risks emerge and technological landscapes evolve, policies laden with complexity become outdated swiftly, rendering them ineffective in addressing emerging vulnerabilities.

The sheer volume of information contained in complex policies can be overwhelming for individuals responsible for implementation. This information overload not only diminishes the likelihood of comprehensive understanding but also increases the chances of essential details being overlooked, leading to potential security gaps.

COMMON USER-MISCONCEPTIONS ABOUT SECURITY

With any shrouded in any form of mystery comes misconceptions and the same is true for Security in GRC. Being an ever-evolving space, it is understably quite hard for everyone to keep up with everything. So, for security efforts to be successful, leaders and practitioners must endeavor to share information and collaborate with users where necessary.

SOME COMMON USER-MISCONCEPTIONS

Misconception #1 : Exclusive IT Responsibility

Users often believe that cybersecurity is solely the domain of the IT department. This misconception leads to a lack of understanding that every individual, regardless of their role, contributes to the overall security posture. Addressing this fallacy requires a cultural shift, emphasizing shared responsibility and the role of each employee in maintaining a secure environment.

Misconception #2: Password Strength Suffices

Users commonly believe that having a strong, unique password is the pinnacle of cybersecurity. However, this overlooks the importance of additional layers such as multi-factor authentication. A detailed explanation of the vulnerabilities associated with password reliance and the enhanced security provided by multi-factor authentication can bridge this knowledge gap.

Misconception #3: Size Equals Safety

There is a prevalent belief, especially among smaller businesses, that they are immune to cyber threats. This misconception arises from the assumption that cybercriminals only target larger entities. A thorough exploration should highlight that smaller organizations are often targeted precisely because of this misconception, necessitating robust security measures regardless of size.

Misconception #4: Set-and-Forget Security

Users may perceive cybersecurity as a one-time setup rather than an ongoing process. Providing detailed insights into the evolving nature of cyber threats, the need for regular updates, and the significance of adapting security measures to emerging risks is crucial. This dispels the notion that once-established security protocols remain effective indefinitely.

Misconception #5: Security vs. Productivity Dilemma

Some users view security measures as impediments to productivity. It's essential to dissect this misconception by illustrating the symbiotic relationship between effective security practices and overall organizational efficiency. Emphasizing how a secure environment enhances, rather than hinders, daily operations encourages a more positive perspective on cybersecurity measures.

By addressing these misconceptions with detailed insights, organizations can foster a nuanced understanding of security principles among users, laying the foundation for a more resilient GRC framework.

THE IMPACT OF JARGON ON POLICY COMPREHENSION

Clear and accessible communication is the first step towards ensuring a successful GRC implementation. Without comprehension, it becomes difficult for users/employees to understand the purpose to be achieved with implemented policies.

A key consideration for the use of jargon in the policy creation process therefore should be put into consideration so the aim of effective GRC is achieved. To have a better understanding of steps to take in order to avoid the potential encumbrances that come with jargons in policy comprehension, let's examine some of the impact it has.

BARRIER TO ENTRY:

Jargon acts as a significant barrier to entry for individuals who may not have a specialized background in cybersecurity or compliance. It creates a divide between experts and non-experts, hindering the latter's ability to comprehend and engage with crucial GRC concepts.

MISINTERPRETATION AND MISCOMMUNICATION:

The use of jargon increases the likelihood of misinterpretation and miscommunication. Non-experts may interpret terms differently, leading to misunderstandings that can have serious consequences in the context of GRC, where precision is paramount.

ALIENATION OF STAKEHOLDER:

The pervasive use of jargon can alienate stakeholders who are essential for effective GRC. Executives, employees, and even external auditors may feel disconnected from the processes and policies if they struggle to understand the language used.

COMPLIANCE CHALLENGES:

Jargon-laden policies and documentation can pose challenges for compliance. If employees cannot decipher the language used, they are more likely to unintentionally violate policies, leading to compliance issues that could have been avoided with clearer communication.

RESISTANCE TO IMPLEMENTATION:

The use of jargon may breed resistance among employees who find it challenging to navigate through complex terms and concepts. This resistance can impede the smooth implementation of GRC measures, as individuals may be less likely to embrace policies that seem convoluted.

LACK OF ACCOUNTABILITY:

When jargon is prevalent, accountability may suffer. If individuals don't fully understand their roles and responsibilities due to complex language, they might not take ownership of GRC tasks, leading to gaps in compliance and risk management.

EDUCATIONAL BARRIERS:

Jargon can create educational barriers, particularly for training programs. When materials are laden with technical terms, it becomes challenging for organizations to effectively educate their workforce on the principles and practices of GRC.

IMPAIRED DECISION-MAKING:

Leaders and decision-makers may struggle to make informed choices when presented with information riddled with jargon. Clear decision-making relies on a comprehensive understanding of risks and compliance, which is hindered when language is overly complex.

INEFFICIENCIES IN INCIDENT RESPONSE:

During incident response scenarios, the use of jargon can slow down the resolution process. Effective communication is crucial in times of crisis, and convoluted language can impede the swift and coordinated response necessary to mitigate risks.

REPUTATION AND TRUST ISSUES:

Excessive use of jargon can erode trust and damage the reputation of GRC initiatives. When stakeholders perceive GRC practices as obscure or incomprehensible, they may question the effectiveness and transparency of the entire system.

THE NEED FOR USER-CENTRIC POLICY LANGUAGE

Advocating for plain language in policy writing is not just a preference; it's a strategic imperative for Governance, Risk, and Compliance (GRC) policy process. Here's why, along with some examples of user-friendly policy language:

ENHANCED COMPREHENSION:

Using plain language ensures that policies are easily understood by a diverse audience, from executives to front-line employees.

Example: Replace complex language like "utilize multi factor authentication" with "use more than one way to prove it's really you."

REDUCED AMBIGUITY:

Plain language reduces ambiguity, leaving little room for misinterpretation or confusion.

Example: Instead of "implement mitigating measures," say "take actions to reduce risks."

IMPROVED ACCESSIBILITY:

Plain language enhances accessibility, making policies inclusive for all, regardless of their level of expertise.

Example: Replace "authorize access" with "give permission to use."

FOSTER COMPLIANCE CULTURE:

User-friendly language fosters a culture of compliance by making expectations clear and approachable.

Example: Instead of "adhere to regulatory requirements," say "follow the rules set by the law."

SIMPLIFIED TECHNICAL TERMS:

Simplifying technical terms makes policies more approachable for non-specialists.

Example: Replace "phishing attacks" with "fake emails trying to trick you."

ACTIVE VOICE AND CLARITY:

Use active voice for clarity and directness in conveying expectations.

Example: Instead of "Access permissions should be requested," say "Ask for permission when you need it."

CONCISENESS AND FOCUS:

Plain language promotes brevity and focus, keeping policies concise and to the point.

Example: Instead of "In the event of a security incident, it is imperative that you promptly report the matter to the designated authority," say "Report security incidents immediately."

REAL-WORLD EXAMPLES:

Integrate real-world examples to illustrate policy points, making them relatable

Example: Instead of "Unauthorized access may result in severe consequences," say "If you snoop into files without permission, you could lose your job."

INTERACTIVE AND ENGAGING LANGUAGE:

Use language that engages the reader, making policies more memorable.

Example: Instead of "Periodic security awareness training is mandatory," say "Let's learn together about staying safe online."

FEEDBACK MECHANISMS:

Encourage feedback by creating policies that invite questions and suggestions.

Example: Instead of "Inquiries should be directed to the designated security officer," say "Have questions? Ask our security expert anytime."

PERSONALIZATION AND CUSTOMIZATION: TAILORING POLICIES TO INDIVIDUAL ROLES

There are several benefits to be reaped from tailoring policies to individual roles. Some of them are:

RELEVANCE AND CONTEXT:

Tailored policies ensure that individuals are presented with guidelines directly relevant to their roles and responsibilities.

Details: For example, a finance department employee may have specific data protection guidelines tailored to financial transactions, while an IT professional may receive policies related to system access and cybersecurity.

ENHANCED COMPLIANCE ADHERENCE:

Employees are more likely to adhere to policies when they perceive them as directly applicable to their daily tasks.

Details: Customized policies reduce ambiguity, making it clearer for employees to understand their compliance obligations within their specific functional contexts.

EFFICIENT TRAINING AND ONBOARDING:

Tailored policies streamline the training process during onboarding, ensuring that hires receive information that is pertinent to their roles.

Details: Instead of overwhelming new employees with a broad set of policies, they receive targeted information, expediting the onboarding process.

RISK MITIGATION:

Customized policies enable a more nuanced approach to risk mitigation, addressing specific vulnerabilities associated with different roles.

Details: For instance, roles dealing with customer data may have heightened security measures compared to roles with less sensitive information, aligning risk mitigation with the potential impact of breaches.

USER EMPOWERMENT:

Tailored policies empower users by acknowledging their distinct roles and responsibilities within the organization.

Details: Employees feel a sense of ownership and accountability when policies are designed with their roles in mind, fostering a proactive and security-conscious culture.

OPTIONS FOR CUSTOMIZABLE SECURITY SETTINGS

Role-Based Access Controls (RBAC): Implement RBAC to assign different levels of access permissions based on job roles. This ensures that individuals have access only to the information and systems necessary for their responsibilities.

Policy Configuration Profiles: Create distinct policy profiles that can be assigned to different roles. These profiles include specific settings and guidelines tailored to the requirements of each role within the organization.

Granular Permission Settings: Offer granular control over permission settings, allowing administrators to customize access levels, data privileges, and security settings based on individual roles.

Adaptive Authentication: Implement adaptive authentication mechanisms that adjust security requirements based on contextual factors such as location, device, and user behavior. This ensures a balance between security and usability tailored to individual roles.

Personalized Training Modules: Develop training modules that are customizable based on job roles. This ensures that employees receive targeted security education relevant to their specific responsibilities.

Incident Response Plans by Role: Tailor incident response plans to different roles, outlining specific procedures and communication protocols. This ensures that individuals know their responsibilities in the event of a security incident

Customizable Security Awareness Campaigns: Design security awareness campaigns that are customizable for different departments or roles. This can include targeted messaging and training materials that address specific security concerns associated with each role.

Role-Specific Compliance Checklists: Develop compliance checklists that are specific to individual roles, outlining the regulatory requirements and best practices relevant to each function within the organization.

CHAPTER 6

Training Vs Culture: Building A Sustainable Cybersecurity Mindset

A cybersecurity mindset refers to the collective awareness, attitudes, and behaviors of individuals within an organization regarding cybersecurity. It encompasses a shared understanding of the importance of cybersecurity, a commitment to best practices, and a proactive approach to mitigating and preventing cyber threats. A strong cybersecurity mindset goes beyond mere compliance with security policies; it reflects a culture where employees are actively engaged in safeguarding digital assets, recognizing the evolving nature of cyber threats, and understanding their role in maintaining a secure environment. This mindset involves continuous learning, adaptability to new security challenges, and a sense of shared responsibility for protecting sensitive information and digital infrastructure. Cultivating a cybersecurity mindset is essential for building resilience against cyber threats and creating a security-conscious organizational culture.

Building a sustainable cybersecurity mindset should be one of the areas any organization puts a lot of dedicated effort into. Let's explore why it matters.

PROACTIVE THREAT MITIGATION:

A cybersecurity mindset empowers individuals to proactively identify and mitigate potential threats before they escalate. This proactive approach is crucial in an environment where cyber threats are continually evolving.

HUMAN-CENTRIC SECURITY:

People are often the first line of defense against cyber threats. Fostering a cybersecurity mindset ensures that individuals understand their role in maintaining security, promoting a human-centric approach to cybersecurity.

ADAPTABILITY TO EMERGING THREATS:

The digital landscape is dynamic, with new threats emerging regularly. A cybersecurity mindset encourages continuous learning and adaptability, enabling individuals to stay informed about the latest threats and adjust their behaviors accordingly.

REDUCTION OF SECURITY INCIDENTS:

A workforce with a strong cybersecurity mindset is less likely to engage in risky behaviors or fall victim to social engineering attacks. This reduction in risky behavior contributes to a decrease in security incidents.

ORGANIZATIONAL RESILIENCE:

A cybersecurity mindset contributes to organizational resilience by creating a culture where employees understand the potential impact of cyber incidents and are prepared to respond effectively. This resilience is vital for minimizing disruption and recovering swiftly from security breaches.

ALIGNMENT WITH REGULATORY REQUIREMENTS:

Many regulatory frameworks and compliance standards emphasize the importance of a security-aware culture. Building a sustainable cybersecurity mindset ensures alignment with these requirements, reducing the risk of non-compliance and associated penalties.

PROTECTION OF SENSITIVE INFORMATION:

Employees with a cybersecurity mindset are more conscientious about protecting sensitive information. This includes customer data, proprietary information, and other important assets that could be targeted by cybercriminals.

COST SAVINGS:

Proactively addressing cybersecurity challenges through a mindset-focused approach can lead to cost savings. By avoiding security incidents and breaches, organizations reduce the financial impact associated with incident response, legal repercussions, and reputational damage.

POSITIVE WORK CULTURE:

A cybersecurity mindset contributes to a positive work culture where employees feel secure and confident in their digital environment. This, in turn, fosters a sense of trust among colleagues and enhances overall job satisfaction.

CUSTOMER AND PARTNER TRUST:

Organizations with a strong cybersecurity mindset convey a commitment to the security and privacy of their stakeholders. This builds trust with customers, partners, and other entities, enhancing the organization's reputation.

COMPETITIVE ADVANTAGE:

In today's interconnected business landscape, organizations that prioritize cybersecurity and instill a cybersecurity mindset gain a competitive advantage. Clients and partners increasingly value working with entities that demonstrate a strong commitment to security.

LONG-TERM SUSTAINABILITY:

Building a sustainable cybersecurity mindset ensures that security practices become ingrained in the organizational culture. It's not a one-time effort but a continuous commitment to maintaining a secure and resilient digital environment over the long term.

AN OVERVIEW OF THE TRAINING VS. CULTURE DILEMMA

The Training vs Culture dilemma in cybersecurity revolves around the challenge of striking the right balance between formal training programs and the broader organizational culture in fostering a secure and sustainable cybersecurity mindset. Here's an overview of this dilemma:

TRAINING COMPONENT

Training programs are designed to impart knowledge, skills, and awareness related to cybersecurity best practices and protocols.

CHARACTERISTICS:

* Structured and targeted sessions.

* Focus on specific skills and technical knowledge.

* Often includes simulated exercises and assessments.

* Measurable outcomes in terms of completion and performance.

Organizational Culture Component:

Organizational culture encompasses the shared values, beliefs, and behaviors of employees regarding cybersecurity. It represents the informal aspects of how security is perceived and integrated into daily operations.

Characteristics:

* Influenced by leadership practices and communication.

* Reflects the collective attitudes and behaviors of employees.

* Emphasizes the everyday application of security principles.

* Difficult to measure directly but manifests in overall behavior.

The Dilemma

Organizations face a dilemma in determining the relative emphasis on formal training versus the development of a security-centric culture. Striking the right balance is challenging, as overreliance on training may result in knowledge decay over time, while overemphasis on culture may lack specificity in addressing evolving cybersecurity threats.

Challenges of Relying Solely on Training:

1. *Knowledge Decay:* Information from training sessions may be forgotten over time, especially if not regularly reinforced.

2. *Lack of Engagement:* Employees may disengage from training if it is perceived as repetitive or irrelevant to their daily tasks.

3. *Addressing Skill Gaps:* Training programs might not effectively bridge skill gaps or provide ongoing skill development.

CHALLENGES OF RELYING SOLELY ON CULTURE:

1. *Time-Intensive:* Developing a robust cybersecurity culture takes time, and immediate results may not be apparent.

2. *Balancing Flexibility and Enforcement:* A strong culture needs to balance flexibility with the enforcement of security policies to avoid becoming too permissive.

3. *Measuring Cultural Impact:* Cultural impact on security metrics can be challenging to measure directly.

STRIKING THE BALANCE:

Organizations must recognize the complementary nature of training and culture. A balanced approach involves integrating regular, targeted training with the cultivation of a security-aware culture. Also, Leadership plays a crucial role in setting the tone for both training initiatives and cultural practices.

FUTURE TRENDS

1. Evolving trends suggest a move toward more interactive and adaptive training methods.

2. The importance of continuous learning aligns with the dynamic nature of cybersecurity threats.

3. Organizations are increasingly recognizing the need for a flexible and adaptive security culture.

KEY CONSIDERATIONS

1. Consider the specific needs and challenges of the organization.

2. Acknowledge that a sustainable cybersecurity mindset requires both formal training and a supportive organizational culture.

3. Regularly assess the effectiveness of both training programs and cultural initiatives.

4. Subsequently, we will take a closer look at some of the concepts highlighted here.

UNDERSTANDING THE TRAINING COMPONENT

It is quite true that not everyone will initially understand the need for ongoing training for cybersecurity professionals but the truth is that just one little deficiency in system fortification or personnel knowledge is sufficient for a cybercriminal to exploit..

While cybersecurity is the job of everybody, the professionals in the field are even more responsible for gaining the requisite knowledge they need to remain ahead of cyber-related criminal efforts.

There are several reasons why it is important for experts in the field to be trained to keep up with new trends that emerge in cybersecurity daily.

1. *Prevention of Cyber Threats:* Cybersecurity training equips employees with the knowledge to recognize and prevent various cyber threats such as phishing, malware, and social engineering attacks. A well-informed workforce serves as a crucial line of defense, preventing the majority of common cyber threats before they can compromise the organization's security.

2. *Mitigation of Insider Threats:* Training raises awareness about potential insider threats, ensuring that employees understand the impact of their actions on cybersecurity. Educated employees are more likely to recognize and report suspicious behavior, mitigating the risks associated with insider threats.

3. *Compliance Adherence:* Cybersecurity training often includes information on regulatory requirements and compliance standards. Ensuring that employees are aware of and adhere to these standards is crucial for avoiding legal consequences and maintaining the organization's reputation.

4. *Adaptability to Evolving Threats:* The cybersecurity landscape is dynamic, with new threats emerging regularly. Training programs provide ongoing education, allowing employees to stay updated on the latest threats and adapt their behavior accordingly.

5. *Enhanced Technical Proficiency:* Cybersecurity training often includes technical skills development, ensuring that employees are proficient in using security tools and protocols. Technical proficiency enhances the organization's overall security posture by enabling employees to effectively implement and manage cybersecurity measures.

6. *Phishing Prevention:* Phishing attacks are a common and potent threat. Training programs teach employees to identify phishing attempts, reducing the likelihood of falling victim to deceptive emails and websites.

7. *Protection of Sensitive Information:* Training emphasizes the importance of protecting sensitive information, including customer data, intellectual property, and proprietary information. Employees who understand the value of this information are more likely to follow security protocols, reducing the risk of data breaches.

8. *Incident Response Preparedness:* Training includes guidelines on how to respond to security incidents. Well-trained employees contribute to an efficient and coordinated incident response, minimizing the impact of security breaches.

9.   *Building a Security-Aware Culture:* Cybersecurity training contributes to the development of a security-aware organizational culture. When security is ingrained in the culture, employees actively contribute to maintaining a secure environment, fostering a sense of shared responsibility.

10. *Reduction in Human Error:* Many security incidents result from unintentional human errors. Training programs aim to reduce these errors by promoting a heightened awareness of security risks and best practices.

11. *Training empowers employees to take an active role in cybersecurity:* When individuals feel capable and knowledgeable, they are more likely to contribute to a security-conscious workplace.

12. *Continuous Learning and Improvement:* Cybersecurity experts are life-long learners. Training programs instill a culture of continuous learning, ensuring that employees are equipped to adapt to new challenges and emerging threats.

SKILL DEVELOPMENT AND TECHNICAL PROFICIENCY AND THE ELEMENTS OF EFFECTIVE CYBERSECURITY TRAINING

This aspect delves into two parts; skill development and technical proficiency, and the elements of effective cybersecurity training. A strategic amalgamation of targeted skill enhancement and meticulous training design is essential for preparing employees to navigate the complexities inherent in digital security.

Let's explore how identifying and honing key cybersecurity skills, coupled with a holistic approach to training, can fortify an organization's defense against emerging threats.

SKILL DEVELOPMENT AND TECHNICAL PROFICIENCY

Identification of Key Cybersecurity Skills: Essential for effective training is understanding which skills are most crucial for your organization. Conduct a comprehensive skills gap analysis to identify areas where employees lack proficiency. This involves assessing the current skills of the workforce against the skills required for cybersecurity roles.

Technical Competencies: Fundamental technical skills form the backbone of cybersecurity roles. Develop a curriculum that covers essential technical competencies such as understanding network protocols, encryption techniques, vulnerability management, and incident response procedures. This may include hands-on labs and practical exercises.

Security Tool Proficiency: Proficiency with security tools is vital for effective cybersecurity operations. Provide hands-on training sessions where employees can become familiar with and proficient in using security tools. This can include antivirus software, intrusion detection systems, and Security Information and Event Management (SIEM) solutions.

Incident Response Training: Knowing how to respond to security incidents is necessary for minimizing potential damage. Develop realistic and scenario-based incident response training. Simulated exercises can help employees practice responding to different types of incidents, ensuring they are well-prepared when faced with a real security event.

Penetration Testing and Ethical Hacking: Understanding how attackers think is essential for effective defense. Introduce ethical hacking and penetration testing training to enhance employees' ability to identify vulnerabilities and understand common attack methodologies. Hands-on labs and practical experiences can be particularly valuable.

Coding and Application Security: Developers need to be aware of secure coding practices to prevent vulnerabilities. Include training on secure coding principles to minimize the risk of security flaws in software applications. This training is crucial for developers to integrate security into the software development lifecycle.

Soft Skills: Effective communication, teamwork, and problem-solving are essential for cybersecurity professionals. Incorporate soft skills development into cybersecurity training programs. This can include exercises and scenarios that enhance communication, collaboration, and critical thinking skills within the security team and across departments.

Regular Training Updates: Cyber threats evolve, and so should employees' skills. Establish a framework for regular updates to training programs. This ensures that employees stay informed about new threats, technologies, and best practices. Continuous learning is key to staying ahead in the dynamic cybersecurity landscape.

Certifications and Recognition: Certifications validate technical proficiency and provide a recognized standard. Encourage employees to pursue relevant cybersecurity certifications. Support their efforts with resources and recognition within the organization, showcasing the value of their expertise.

ELEMENTS OF EFFECTIVE CYBERSECURITY TRAINING

1. *Customization Based on Roles:* One-size-fits-all training may not be as effective as role-specific training. Tailor training programs to the specific roles and responsibilities of employees. This ensures that the content is relevant to their daily tasks and challenges.

2. *Interactive Learning Methods:* Passive learning may result in lower engagement and retention. Incorporate interactive elements such as simulations, hands-on exercises, and case studies. Interactive learning methods keep participants engaged and allow them to apply theoretical knowledge in practical scenarios.

3. *Realistic Scenarios and Simulations:* Simulating real-world scenarios enhances practical skills and preparedness. Develop realistic simulations of cyber threats and incidents. These simulations can provide employees with hands-on experience in a controlled environment, allowing them to practice responding to various cybersecurity challenges.

4. *Continuous Assessment and Feedback:* Regular assessment ensures that employees grasp the material effectively. Incorporate quizzes, assessments, and feedback mechanisms throughout the training. This ongoing evaluation helps gauge understanding and provides constructive feedback to reinforce learning.

5. *Multimodal Delivery:* People have different learning preferences. Offer training content in various formats, including videos, written materials, interactive modules, and live sessions. This accommodates diverse learning styles and ensures that participants can engage with the material in a way that suits them best.

6. *Accessible Training Materials:* Accessibility ensures that all employees can participate in training. Provide training materials in accessible formats, considering factors such as readability, compatibility with assistive technologies, and language clarity. This ensures that everyone, regardless of their abilities, can benefit from the training.

7. *Reinforcement and Refresher Courses:* Continuous reinforcement is essential to combat knowledge decay. Schedule regular refresher courses or briefings to reinforce key concepts. This helps employees stay current with cybersecurity best practices and updates, reducing the risk of forgetting crucial information over time.

8. *Leadership Support and Involvement:* Leadership commitment signals the importance of cybersecurity to the entire organization. Ensure leadership involvement in training initiatives. This can include executives participating in training sessions, communicating the importance of cybersecurity, and demonstrating a commitment to security practices.

9. *User-friendly platforms enhance the learning experience:* Invest in learning management systems (LMS) or platforms that are intuitive, easy to navigate, and provide a positive user experience. A user-friendly interface encourages active participation and makes the learning process more enjoyable.

10. *Metrics and Evaluation:* Metrics help assess the effectiveness of training programs. Establish key performance indicators (KPIs) to measure the impact of training on cybersecurity outcomes. This could include tracking incident reduction, improved incident response times, and the overall improvement in employees' ability to handle cybersecurity challenges.

THE ROLE OF ORGANIZATIONAL CULTURE

ORGANIZATIONAL CULTURE AS A CONCEPT IN CYBERSECURITY

Cybersecurity culture refers to the shared values, beliefs, attitudes, and behaviors within an organization concerning the importance of cybersecurity. It represents the collective mindset of individuals within the organization regarding the protection of digital assets, sensitive information, and the overall resilience against cyber threats.

A strong cybersecurity culture goes beyond mere compliance with security policies and regulations. It involves fostering a sense of shared responsibility among employees at all levels, promoting awareness of cyber risks, and encouraging proactive measures to mitigate potential threats. In a cybersecurity-aware culture, individuals understand the impact of their actions on the organization's security posture and actively contribute to maintaining a secure digital environment.

Key elements of a robust cybersecurity culture include:

1. *Awareness*: Employees are well-informed about cybersecurity risks, best practices, and the potential consequences of security incidents.

2. *Responsibility*: There is a shared sense of responsibility for cybersecurity, where individuals understand their role in safeguarding digital assets and sensitive information.

3. *Proactivity*: The culture encourages a proactive approach to identifying and addressing potential cyber threats, rather than a reactive stance after an incident occurs.

4. *Continuous Learning:* There is an emphasis on continuous learning and staying updated on the evolving landscape of cyber threats and security measures.

5. *Collaboration:* Departments and individuals collaborate seamlessly to address cybersecurity challenges, fostering a holistic and organization-wide approach.

6. *Leadership Support:* Leadership actively supports and prioritizes cybersecurity initiatives, setting the tone for the entire organization.

7. *Adaptability:* The culture is adaptable to changes in technology, regulations, and emerging threats, ensuring that security measures remain effective over time.

8. *Incident Response Preparedness:* The organization is prepared to respond effectively to security incidents, with well-defined incident response plans and a focus on minimizing the impact of breaches.

Training Vs Culture Dilemma: Striking The Balance

CHALLENGES OF RELYING SOLELY ON TRAINING

Here we will take a look at three challenges of relying solely on training; knowledge decay over time, lack of employee engagement and addressing skill gaps.

1. *Knowledge Decay Over Time:* Employees may forget crucial information over time if it's not consistently reinforced or updated. This decay in knowledge can lead to outdated practices and increased vulnerability to security risks.

   Implications

   * Reduced effectiveness of cybersecurity measures due to forgotten information.

   * Increased risk of using obsolete or insecure practices.

   Mitigation Strategies

   * Regularly provide refresher courses or updates to training programs to reinforce key concepts.

* Encourage continuous learning through ongoing educational initiatives and resources.

* Provide access to up-to-date materials and resources for self-directed learning.

2. *Lack of Employee Engagement:* Training sessions that are perceived as dull, irrelevant, or time-consuming may result in low engagement levels among employees.

Implications:

* Disengaged employees are less likely to retain information and apply best practices.

* A lack of interest in training may lead to a culture where security is not prioritized.

Mitigation Strategies:

* Incorporate interactive elements into training, such as simulations, hands-on exercises, and real-world scenarios.

* Customize training content to align with employees' roles, making it more relevant to their daily tasks.

* Communicate the importance of security and how it directly relates to individual and organizational well-being.

3. *Addressing Skill Gaps:* Training programs may not effectively bridge existing skill gaps among employees, especially if the gap is significant or if the training content is not tailored to specific needs.

Implications:

* Unaddressed skill gaps can result in suboptimal implementation of practices, leaving vulnerabilities unattended.

* Employees may feel overwhelmed or frustrated if training does not adequately address their skill development needs.

Mitigation Strategies:

* Conduct a thorough skills gap analysis to identify areas that need targeted training.

* Provide personalized training plans that address individual skill gaps and align with career development goals.

* Offer hands-on training and practical exercises to reinforce theoretical knowledge and enhance practical skills.

CHALLENGES OF RELYING SOLELY ON CULTURE

Let's examine the challenges of relying solely on culture in terms of culture taking time to develop, balancing flexibility and enforcement and measuring cultural impact on security metrics. Building a robust security culture is a gradual process that requires time and consistent effort.

Implications:

* Immediate results may not be apparent, leading to potential security vulnerabilities during the culture development phase.

* Employees might not fully embrace the desired security behaviors until the culture is firmly established.

Mitigation Strategies:

* Foster a culture of security awareness from the outset, emphasizing its importance.

* Provide ongoing communication and support to encourage the gradual adoption of security-conscious behaviors.

* Incorporate security into the onboarding process for new employees to expedite cultural integration.

BALANCING FLEXIBILITY AND ENFORCEMENT

Striking the right balance between a flexible and enforceable security culture can be challenging. Overemphasis on strict enforcement may create resistance among employees, leading to non-compliance or resentment. It may result in inconsistent security practices, leaving the organization vulnerable.

Mitigation Strategies:

* Develop clear and reasonable security policies that strike a balance between flexibility and enforceability.

* Foster a culture of open communication, allowing employees to provide feedback on security policies.

* Regularly review and update security policies to ensure they remain relevant and reasonable.

MEASURING CULTURAL IMPACT ON SECURITY METRICS

Quantifying the impact of a security culture on measurable security metrics requires some stealth work as there are challenges that may arise in the process.

Implications:

* Difficulty in assessing the effectiveness of the security culture in tangible terms.

* Lack of concrete data may hinder the organization's ability to gauge improvements or areas that need attention.

Mitigation Strategies:

* Develop key performance indicators (KPIs) aligned with security culture goals.

* Implement regular assessments or surveys to gather qualitative data on the employees' perception of the security culture.

* Correlate security incidents and breaches with cultural initiatives to identify patterns and measure the impact over time.

ORGANIZATIONS WITH SUCCESSFUL TRAINING PROGRAMMES AND CYBERSECURITY CULTURES AND HOW THEY DO IT

Several organizations are recognized for their successful training programs in cybersecurity. Their approaches encompass a combination of interactive learning, real-world simulations, and continuous updates to keep employees informed. Here are a few examples:

GOOGLE

Training Focus: Google places a strong emphasis on continuous training and development for its employees, including cybersecurity awareness.

Approach: They use a combination of interactive training modules, simulated phishing exercises, and real-world scenario-based learning.

Outcome: Google's proactive training approach has contributed to a security-aware culture, reducing the risk of phishing attacks and other security incidents.

Security as a Priority: Google places security as a top organizational priority. This commitment is communicated from leadership to every employee, creating a culture where security is ingrained in day-to-day operations.

Innovation and Adaptability: The company fosters a culture of innovation and adaptability, allowing for quick responses to emerging threats and the development of cutting-edge security solutions.

MICROSOFT

Training Focus: Microsoft is committed to educating its employees about evolving cybersecurity threats.

Approach: They provide a variety of training resources, including role-specific security training, simulated cyber-attacks, and access to cybersecurity experts for continuous learning.

Outcome: Microsoft's training initiatives have led to a more security-conscious workforce, with employees actively participating in the protection of digital assets.

Cultural Practices: Shared Responsibility: Microsoft emphasizes that cybersecurity is a shared responsibility across all levels of the organization. This encourages employees to actively contribute to security measures.

Continuous Learning: The company promotes a culture of continuous learning, offering various resources, including role-specific training, simulated cyber-attacks, and access to cybersecurity experts.

JPMORGAN CHASE

Training Focus: JPMorgan Chase recognizes the importance of cybersecurity in the financial sector and invests significantly in employee training.

Approach: Their training programs cover a range of topics, from basic security hygiene to advanced threat detection and response.

Outcome: JPMorgan Chase has seen a reduction in security incidents and improved incident response times, attributed to the effectiveness of their training initiatives.

Cultural Practices: Leadership Commitment: JPMorgan Chase exhibits strong leadership commitment to cybersecurity. This commitment sets the tone for the entire organization, signaling the importance of security practices.

Customer Trust: The organization emphasizes the importance of protecting customer data, instilling a sense of responsibility among employees to maintain the trust of clients.

Cisco

Training Focus: As a leading cybersecurity solutions provider, Cisco prioritizes comprehensive training for its employees.

Approach: Cisco offers a Cybersecurity Scholarship program, hands-on training labs, and certifications to enhance the technical skills of its workforce.

Outcome: The training programs contribute to a workforce that is well-versed in cybersecurity principles, supporting Cisco's commitment to providing secure solutions to its clients.

Cultural Practices: Collaboration: Cisco promotes collaboration among different departments, creating a cross-functional approach to cybersecurity. This ensures that security is integrated into every aspect of the business.

Continuous Improvement: Cisco's culture encourages continuous improvement in security practices. Regular evaluations and updates to security protocols help the organization stay ahead of evolving threats.

IBM

Training Focus: IBM recognizes the dynamic nature of cybersecurity and invests in ongoing education for its employees.

Approach: IBM offers a range of training programs, including virtual labs, interactive modules, and industry-recognized certifications.

Outcome: IBM's training initiatives contribute to a workforce that is adaptive to emerging threats and well-prepared to address complex cybersecurity challenges.

Cultural Practices: Adaptability and Flexibility: IBM's culture promotes adaptability and flexibility in the face of evolving threats. This cultural aspect allows the organization to adjust its security strategies promptly.

Empowering Employees: IBM empowers its employees to be proactive in cybersecurity. This includes encouraging a mindset of "see something, say something," fostering open communication about potential security issues.

FUTURE TRENDS IN CYBERSECURITY EDUCATION

The future holds a lot of prospects for all aspects of our lives and education in cybersecurity is not left out either. New training methodologies especially in technology provide a great opportunity for effective education for security professionals. Some of this trends include:

IMMERSIVE TECHNOLOGIES (VR AND AR):

Virtual Reality (VR) and Augmented Reality (AR) are being incorporated into cybersecurity training to create immersive simulations. These technologies provide realistic environments for hands-on learning.

Benefits: Enhances situational awareness, allows for realistic training scenarios, and provides a safe space to practice without real-world consequences.

Cyber Range Platforms:

Cyber range platforms offer virtual environments where participants can practice defending against simulated cyber attacks. These platforms replicate the complexity of actual networks and systems.

Benefits: Provides hands-on experience in a risk-free environment, facilitates team collaboration, and allows for the testing of various cybersecurity skills.

AI-Driven Training Tools:

Artificial Intelligence (AI) is being used to analyze individual learning patterns and customize training content accordingly. AI-driven tools can also simulate evolving cyber threats for training purposes.

Benefits: Enhances personalization, adapts to learners' needs, and provides dynamic content to address the latest cybersecurity challenges.

Cloud-Based Training Platforms:

Cloud-based training platforms offer flexibility in accessing training materials from anywhere, at any time. These platforms often include collaborative features for team-based learning.

Benefits: Facilitates remote learning, allows for seamless collaboration, and ensures easy access to updated training resources.

Capture The Flag (CTF) Platforms:

CTF platforms provide gamified cybersecurity challenges where participants must solve security-related puzzles and scenarios. These platforms are widely used for hands-on training.

Benefits: Develops practical skills, encourages problem-solving, and offers a dynamic and engaging learning experience.

INTEGRATION OF TRAINING AND TECHNOLOGIES

Blended Learning Approaches: Combining traditional classroom training with online modules, simulations, and hands-on exercises to create a comprehensive and adaptive learning experience.

Benefits: Maximizes flexibility, accommodates different learning styles, and leverages the strengths of various training methods.

Continuous Assessment and Feedback: Utilizing technology to implement continuous assessment mechanisms, including quizzes, simulations, and real-time feedback loops. This ensures that learners receive timely information on their progress.

Benefits: Promotes ongoing improvement, identifies areas for further training, and reinforces positive learning behaviors.

Mobile Learning Applications: Mobile applications allow learners to access training content on their smartphones or tablets. These apps often provide on-the-go learning opportunities and can include features like push notifications for reminders.

Benefits: Facilitates learning at the learner's convenience, supports just-in-time learning, and accommodates diverse learning environments.

Data Analytics for Learning Insights: Leveraging data analytics to gather insights into learner performance, engagement, and areas that may need additional focus. Analytics inform adjustments to training strategies based on empirical data.

Benefits: Enables evidence-based decision-making, identifies trends, and allows for continuous improvement of training programs.

Anticipated Challenges In Trends In Cybersecurity Education

Anticipating challenges in the future trends of cybersecurity education is crucial for preparing effective strategies to overcome them. Let's look at some anticipated challenge:

Rapidly Evolving Threat Landscape: The cybersecurity landscape is dynamic, with new threats emerging continuously. Keeping educational content up-to-date with the latest threats, attack vectors, and defense strategies is a perpetual challenge.

Skill Gap Widening: The demand for cybersecurity professionals is growing faster than the supply. Bridging the skill gap requires innovative educational approaches and collaboration between academia and industry to ensure graduates are job-ready.

Integration of Emerging Technologies: Integrating emerging technologies like artificial intelligence, machine learning, blockchain, and quantum computing into cybersecurity education is essential. However, developing relevant curricula and resources for these technologies poses a challenge.

Diversity and Inclusion: Achieving diversity and inclusion in cybersecurity education remains a challenge. Encouraging underrepresented groups to pursue cybersecurity careers requires addressing biases, providing equitable opportunities, and fostering inclusive learning environments.

Global Collaboration and Standardization: Cyber threats are global, and educational efforts need to be coordinated globally. Establishing standards and frameworks for cybersecurity education that are recognized internationally is challenging but essential for a unified response to cyber threats.

Continuous Training and Lifelong Learning: Cybersecurity professionals need continuous training to stay updated with evolving threats. Implementing lifelong learning initiatives and providing accessible, ongoing training opportunities is a challenge in traditional education structures.

Adapting to Remote Learning: The shift to remote learning, accelerated by global events, presents challenges in providing hands-on, practical experiences traditionally obtained in physical labs. Ensuring the effectiveness of remote learning tools and maintaining student engagement is vital.

Cybersecurity Awareness: Building a cybersecurity-aware culture among the general population is challenging. Educating individuals about basic cybersecurity hygiene and the importance of online safety is an ongoing struggle.

Legal and Ethical Education: Incorporating legal and ethical considerations into cybersecurity education is crucial. Understanding the legal implications of cybersecurity actions and ethical decision-making in complex scenarios is a challenge for educators.

Cost of Cybersecurity Education: High costs associated with cybersecurity education, including training programs, certifications, and specialized courses, can create barriers for individuals seeking to enter the field. Finding ways to make education more accessible is a significant challenge.

Threat Intelligence Integration: Integrating threat intelligence into educational programs is vital for preparing students for real-world scenarios. However, ensuring that students have access to relevant, timely, and accurate threat intelligence is challenging due to the rapidly changing threat landscape.

Privacy Concerns: Addressing privacy concerns in cybersecurity education, especially when using real-world datasets or scenarios, requires careful consideration. Balancing the need for practical experience with ethical and privacy considerations is a challenge.

Dynamic Regulatory Landscape: The regulatory landscape for cybersecurity is dynamic and varies across regions. Educators must keep abreast of changes in regulations and ensure that educational programs align with legal requirements.

Cybersecurity Education for Non-Technical Roles: As cybersecurity becomes a concern for roles beyond technical positions, developing effective cybersecurity education for non-technical roles poses a challenge. Tailoring content for diverse job functions is essential.

Addressing these challenges requires collaboration among educational institutions, industry, and regulatory bodies. Flexibility, adaptability, and a commitment to staying current with industry trends will be key to overcoming these challenges in the future of cybersecurity education.

Insider Threat: Recognizing and Mitigating Human Risk From Within

What Does Insider Threats Mean?

An insider threat refers to the potential for an individual within an organization, such as an employee, contractor, or business partner, to misuse their authorized access to data, systems, or networks with malicious intent or negligence. Insider threats can pose significant risks to an organization's cybersecurity, data integrity, and overall security posture. It's important to recognize that not all insider threats are malicious; some may result from unintentional actions or negligence.

A research independently conducted by Ponemon Institute found that," Malicious, negligent and compromised users are a serious and growing risk. As the 2022 Cost of Insider Threats: Global Report reveals, insider threat incidents have risen 44% over the past two years, with costs per incident up more than a third to $15.38 million. Also:

* The cost of credential theft to organizations increased 65% from $2.79 million in 2020 to $4.6 million at present.

* The time to contain an insider threat incident increased from 77 days to 85 days, leading organizations to spend the most on containment.

* Incidents that took more than 90 days to contain cost organizations an average of $17.19 million on an annualized basis.

Key components of the definition of insider threats include:

Authorized Access: Insider threats involve individuals who have legitimate access to an organization's internal resources, systems, or sensitive information as part of their job responsibilities. This access is typically granted to perform their duties effectively.

Malicious Intent or Negligence: Insider threats can manifest in two primary forms:

a. *Malicious Insider Threats:* These involve individuals who intentionally misuse their authorized access for personal gain, to harm the organization, or to engage in activities detrimental to security.

b. *Unintentional Insider Threats:* These result from employees or individuals who, without malicious intent, inadvertently compromise security through actions such as falling victim to phishing attacks or mishandling sensitive information.

The definition emphasizes the potential harm that insider threats can inflict on an organization. This harm may include data breaches, theft of intellectual property, unauthorized access, disclosure of sensitive information, or disruption of operations.

Malicious insiders may have diverse motivations, such as financial gain, revenge, ideological reasons, or a desire to sabotage operations. Understanding these motivations is crucial for developing effective mitigation strategies.

INSIDER THREAT LIFECYCLE

Insider threats can be viewed through a life cycle that includes recruitment, insider activity, and detection. Recognizing the stages of the lifecycle is essential for implementing proactive measures to identify and mitigate threats at an early stage.

MITIGATION AND PREVENTION:

Organizations need to implement measures to mitigate the risk of insider threats. This involves a combination of technical controls, such as access monitoring and data loss prevention tools, as well as non-technical measures, such as security awareness training and fostering a culture of security.

Continuous Monitoring: Insider threats require ongoing attention and monitoring. As the threat landscape evolves, organizations need to adapt their strategies to detect and respond to emerging insider threats effectively.

Contextual Understanding: Recognizing that not all insider threats are intentional helps organizations approach the issue with a balanced perspective. Unintentional mistakes, such as accidental data disclosures or misconfigurations, can also result in security incidents.

Understanding the definition of insider threats is foundational to developing comprehensive strategies for prevention, detection, and response. It involves a holistic approach that combines technological solutions, employee education, and proactive monitoring to safeguard against the diverse and evolving nature of insider threats.

Addressing insider threats is of paramount significance for organizations due to the potential harm and risks they pose. The following points highlight the importance of actively managing and mitigating insider threats:

1. **Data Protection:**

   Risk to Sensitive Information: Insiders with malicious intent can access, manipulate, or exfiltrate sensitive data, including intellectual property, customer information, or proprietary business processes. Addressing insider threats is crucial to protect crucial data assets.

2. **Cybersecurity Resilience:**

   Strengthening Defenses: By recognizing and mitigating insider threats, organizations enhance their overall cybersecurity resilience. This includes protecting against both intentional attacks by malicious insiders and unintentional vulnerabilities introduced by well-meaning employees.

3. **Financial Impact:**

   Mitigating Financial Losses: Insider threats can result in significant financial losses, including costs associated with data breaches, legal actions, and reputation damage. Proactive measures to address insider threats help minimize the financial impact on the organization.

4. **Reputation Management:**

   Preserving Trust: Security incidents caused by insiders can erode trust among customers, partners, and stakeholders. Addressing insider threats is crucial for preserving the organization's reputation and maintaining trust in the marketplace.

5. **Intellectual Property Protection:**

Safeguarding Innovation: For many organizations, intellectual property is a key differentiator and a source of competitive advantage. Mitigating insider threats is essential to protect proprietary information and maintain a competitive edge.

6. **Compliance and Legal Obligations:**

Meeting Regulatory Requirements: Many industries have strict regulations regarding data protection and privacy. Addressing insider threats is essential for organizations to comply with these regulations and fulfill their legal obligations.

7. **Operational Continuity:**

Preventing Disruptions: Insider threats can disrupt normal business operations, leading to downtime and financial losses. Implementing measures to address insider threats contributes to operational continuity and business resilience.

8. **Insider Trading Prevention:**

Ensuring Fair Practices: In financial and regulated industries, addressing insider threats is crucial to prevent insider trading. This involves securing sensitive financial information and ensuring fair and transparent market practices.

9. **Employee Trust and Morale:**

Maintaining a Positive Workplace: Proactively addressing insider threats helps create a workplace environment where employees feel secure and trust that their colleagues are committed to ethical conduct. This positively impacts morale and organizational culture.

MALICIOUS INSIDERS VS UNINTENTIONAL INSIDERS

Understanding the distinction between malicious insiders and unintentional insiders is crucial for developing effective strategies to address insider threats. Both types of insider threats pose risks to an organization's cybersecurity, but they differ in their motivations and behaviors.

WHO ARE MALICIOUS INSIDERS?

Malicious insiders are individuals within an organization who intentionally and knowingly engage in activities that harm the organization's security, integrity, or confidentiality. Their actions are driven by malicious intent, often with the goal of personal gain or causing harm to the organization.

Malicious insiders may be motivated by various factors, including:

    a. *Financial Gain:* Stealing sensitive information for personal financial benefit.

    b. *Revenge:* Seeking retaliation for perceived grievances or disagreements.

    c. *Espionage:* Working on behalf of external entities to steal intellectual property or proprietary information.

    d. *Sabotage:* Intentionally disrupting operations, networks, or systems.

CHARACTERISTICS OF A MALICIOUS INSIDER

Malicious insiders often exhibit traits such as:

    a. *Deception:* Engaging in covert actions to hide their malicious activities.

    b. *Intentional Evasion:* Attempting to bypass security controls deliberately.

c. *Sophistication:* Some malicious insiders possess a high level of technical knowledge to carry out complex attacks.

Examples of malicious insider actions include:

a. Unauthorized access to sensitive databases.

b. Theft of proprietary information or intellectual property.

c. Intentional introduction of malware or malicious code.

d. Sabotage of systems or networks.

DETECTION CHALLENGE

Detecting malicious insiders can be challenging because they may have legitimate access to systems and data. Behavioral analysis, anomaly detection, and monitoring for suspicious activities are key to identification.

UNINTENTIONAL INSIDERS

Unintentional insiders are individuals within an organization who, without malicious intent, inadvertently compromise security through their actions. These actions may result from mistakes, lack of awareness, or negligence regarding security best practices. Unintentional insiders are not driven by malicious intent. Their actions are typically a result of:

a. *Lack of Security Awareness:* Unintentional insiders may not be fully aware of the security implications of their actions.

b. Human Error: Mistakes such as misconfigurations, accidental data disclosures, or falling victim to phishing attacks.

Characteristics of An Unintentional Insider

Unintentional insiders may display characteristics like:

a. *Lack of Malice:* Their actions are not intended to harm the organization.

b. Unawareness: Limited understanding of cybersecurity best practices.

c. Negligence: Unintentional insiders may neglect security protocols due to oversight or lack of training.

Examples of unintentional insider actions include:

a. Accidental sharing of sensitive information.

b. Falling victim to phishing attacks and disclosing login credentials.

c. Misconfigurations of security settings.

d. Failure to apply software updates, leading to vulnerabilities.

DETECTION CHALLENGES

Detecting unintentional insiders often involves monitoring for anomalies and deviations from established security policies. Training and awareness programs are crucial for reducing the likelihood of unintentional insider incidents.

MITIGATING STRATEGIES

The kind of mitigating strategy an organization would need to deploy on insider threats will largely depend on the kind of threat the insider is.

MITIGATING STRATEGIES FOR MALICIOUS INSIDERS

a. *Access Controls:* Implement stringent access controls to limit the potential damage malicious insiders can inflict.

b. *Behavioral Analysis:* Employ behavioral analytics to detect abnormal patterns of activity.

c. *Whistleblower Programs:* Encourage a culture where employees feel comfortable reporting suspicious activities.

MITIGATING STRATEGIES FOR UNINTENTIONAL INSIDERS

a. *Security Training:* Provide comprehensive security training to educate employees on best practices and potential risks.

b. *User Awareness Programs:* Regularly communicate security policies and reinforce awareness of common threats.

c. *Technology Safeguards*: Implement technologies like data loss prevention (DLP) to prevent accidental data disclosures.

COMMON MOTIVATIONS BEHIND INSIDER THREATS

Insider threats can arise from various motivations, and understanding these motivations is crucial for organizations to implement effective strategies to mitigate the risks posed by insiders. Common motivations behind insider threats include:

1. *Financial Gain:* Some insiders are motivated by the prospect of financial benefit. This can involve selling sensitive information, intellectual property, or trade secrets to external parties for personal profit.

Indicators: Unexplained lifestyle changes, sudden wealth, or financial troubles can be indicators of an insider seeking financial gain.

2. ***Revenge or Retaliation:*** Employees who feel wronged, overlooked, or mistreated within the organization may resort to insider threats as a form of revenge. This can include actions that harm the organization or specific individuals.

Indicators: Expressions of dissatisfaction, conflicts with colleagues, or a history of grievances may signal potential insider threats motivated by revenge.

3. ***Ideological or Political Beliefs:*** Insiders may act based on personal beliefs, ideologies, or political motivations. This can include actions intended to further a cause, promote a particular agenda, or sabotage an organization for ideological reasons.

Indicators: Expressions of strong ideological or political views, affiliations with extremist groups, or participation in activism may be red flags.

4. ***Espionage or Competitive Advantage:*** Insiders may be motivated by the desire to gain a competitive advantage or to engage in corporate espionage. This involves stealing proprietary information, business plans, or intellectual property for the benefit of a competitor.

Indicators: Unusual interest in competitors, attempts to access sensitive business plans, or unexplained communications with external entities may indicate espionage motives.

5. ***Career Frustration or Discontent:*** Insiders experiencing dissatisfaction with their career, promotions, or work environment may resort to insider threats as a way to express discontent or seek opportunities elsewhere.

Indicators: Frequent expressions of frustration, resentment towards management, or an observable decline in work performance may suggest potential insider threats.

6. ***Accidental or Negligent Actions:*** Not all insider threats are intentional. Some arise from employees' unintentional actions or negligence, such as clicking on phishing emails, misconfiguration of security settings, or mishandling sensitive information.

   Indicators: Lack of awareness about security best practices, frequent mistakes, or failure to follow established protocols may lead to unintentional insider threats.

7. ***Personal Issues or Extortion:*** Personal issues, such as financial problems, addiction, or personal conflicts, may drive insiders to engage in malicious activities. Extortion, where an insider seeks to exploit sensitive information for personal gain, is also a motivating factor.

   Indicators: Noticeable personal challenges, unusual requests for access or information, or involvement in suspicious external activities may be signs of personal motivation.

8. ***Loyalty to External Entities:*** Insiders may be motivated by loyalty to external entities, such as competitors or threat actors. This can involve providing access to systems, sharing confidential information, or actively collaborating with external parties.

   Indicators: Unusual connections with external entities, suspicious communications, or activities inconsistent with job responsibilities may indicate loyalty-driven motivations.

THE PROFILE OF AN INSIDER THREAT: RECOGNIZING BEHAVIOURAL INDICATORS

Behavioral changes or patterns can serve as early warning signs that an employee may be engaging in activities that pose a risk to cybersecurity. Here are key behavioral indicators that organizations should be attentive to and the reasoning behind them:

Sudden Changes in Work Habits:

Indicator: Abrupt alterations in an employee's work habits, including irregular working hours, increased or decreased productivity, or a decline in job performance.

Reasoning: Insiders may modify their work habits to facilitate unauthorized activities without attracting attention.

Unusual Access Patterns:

Indicator: Unexplained or irregular access to sensitive systems, databases, or files, especially outside of an employee's normal job responsibilities.

Reasoning: Insiders seeking to exploit their access may exhibit unusual patterns to conduct malicious activities discreetly.

Excessive Use of Privileges:

Indicator: Employees leveraging their privileges excessively, attempting to access information beyond their role requirements, or making unauthorized changes to systems or data.

Reasoning: Malicious insiders often exploit their authorized access to carry out unauthorized activities.

Lack of Team Collaboration:

Indicator: Withdrawal from team collaboration, avoidance of colleagues, or a sudden decline in communication with coworkers.

Reasoning: Insiders involved in malicious activities may distance themselves to avoid detection or interference.

Unexplained Wealth or Financial Issues:

Indicator: A noticeable change in an employee's financial situation, such as sudden wealth, financial troubles, or living beyond their means.

Reasoning: Insiders motivated by financial gain may display indicators related to their changing financial circumstances.

Frequent Violations of Policies:

Indicator: Repeated violations of organizational policies, especially those related to data handling, access control, or security protocols.

Reasoning: Insiders may intentionally breach policies to achieve their objectives or exploit vulnerabilities.

Erosion of Trust:

Indicator: A noticeable decline in trust among team members, strained relationships, or a general atmosphere of distrust within the organization.

Reasoning: Malicious insiders may erode trust intentionally or create discord to distract from their activities.

Unusual Interactions with External Entities:

Indicator: Suspicious communications or interactions with external entities, particularly competitors or unauthorized third parties.

Reasoning: Insiders with malicious intent may collaborate with external entities for financial gain or to further their goals.

Repeated Security Violations:

Indicator: Consistent violation of security protocols, such as sharing passwords, bypassing security controls, or attempting unauthorized access.

Reasoning: Insiders may intentionally compromise security measures to facilitate their activities.

Changes in Personal Behavior:

Indicator: Observable changes in an employee's personal behavior, demeanor, or attitude, such as increased stress, anxiety, or signs of emotional distress.

Reasoning: Personal issues or emotional strain may drive individuals to engage in malicious activities.

Unauthorized Data Exfiltration Attempts:

Indicator: Unexplained attempts to transfer or download large amounts of sensitive data, especially if such actions are outside the scope of an employee's role.

Reasoning: Malicious insiders may attempt to steal or leak sensitive information for personal gain or external collaboration.

Resistance to Change:

Indicator: Strong resistance to changes in security measures, policy updates, or system modifications.

Reasoning: Insiders may resist changes that hinder their ability to carry out malicious activities undetected.

Insider Threat Risk Factors

Insider threat risk factors are characteristics or conditions that increase the likelihood of an insider engaging in activities that pose a threat to an organization's security. Recognizing these risk factors is essential for implementing effective preventive measures and mitigating the potential impact of insider threats. Here are key insider threat risk factors:

Access Privileges:

Risk Factor: Employees with excessive access privileges, especially those beyond their job responsibilities, are at a higher risk of becoming insider threats. This includes individuals with privileged access to sensitive data or systems.

Reasoning: The more extensive an employee's access, the greater the potential for misuse or exploitation.

Job Dissatisfaction:

Risk Factor: Disgruntled or dissatisfied employees may be more inclined to engage in malicious activities as a form of retaliation or expression of frustration.

Reasoning: Job dissatisfaction can lead to a negative outlook, reducing loyalty and increasing the likelihood of insider threats.

Financial Issues:

Risk Factor: Employees facing financial difficulties, debts, or other economic challenges may be susceptible to bribery, coercion, or may seek financial gain through unauthorized activities.

Reasoning: Financial stress can motivate employees to compromise their ethical standards for personal financial relief.

Lack of Security Awareness:

Risk Factor: Employees who are not adequately educated about security risks, policies, and best practices are more likely to inadvertently engage in activities that compromise security.

Reasoning: Lack of awareness increases the likelihood of falling victim to phishing, social engineering, or other manipulation techniques.

Poor Work Relationships:

Risk Factor: Individuals experiencing conflict or strained relationships with colleagues, supervisors, or the organization are at an increased risk of becoming insider threats.

Reasoning: Strained relationships may lead to intentional harm or malicious actions as a form of retaliation.

Past Incidents or Disciplinary Actions:

Risk Factor: Employees with a history of disciplinary actions, security incidents, or policy violations may pose an increased risk of engaging in future insider threats.

Reasoning: Past incidents may indicate a pattern of behavior that warrants close monitoring.

Unrestricted Internet Access:

Risk Factor: Allowing employees unrestricted access to the internet may expose them to external influences, increasing the risk of falling victim to social engineering attacks or being recruited by external threat actors.

Reasoning: Unrestricted access provides more opportunities for employees to be targeted or manipulated.

Inadequate Monitoring and Auditing:

Risk Factor: Lack of robust monitoring and auditing practices makes it difficult to detect unusual or suspicious behavior, allowing insider threats to go unnoticed.

Reasoning: Without effective monitoring, malicious activities may occur without timely intervention.

Organizational Changes:

Risk Factor: Major organizational changes, such as mergers, acquisitions, layoffs, or restructuring, can create uncertainty and stress, potentially leading employees to become disgruntled or more susceptible to external recruitment.

Reasoning: Changes in the workplace environment may contribute to increased insider threat risk.

Remote Work Challenges:

Risk Factor: The shift to remote work introduces challenges related to monitoring and controlling employee activities, potentially making it easier for insiders to engage in malicious activities undetected.

Reasoning: Remote work environments may lack the same level of oversight as traditional office settings.

Third-Party Relationships:

Risk Factor: Employees who have connections or affiliations with external entities, such as competitors, may pose an increased risk of insider threats, especially if loyalty is divided.

Reasoning: External relationships may create opportunities for collaboration or exploitation.

Lack of Employee Engagement:

Risk Factor: Employees who feel disengaged or undervalued may be less invested in the success of the organization, increasing the likelihood of insider threats.

Reasoning: Lack of engagement may lead to a diminished sense of loyalty and commitment.

INSIDER THREAT INCIDENTS: REAL-WORLD EXAMPLES

EDWARD SNOWDEN (2013):

Edward Snowden, a former National Security Agency (NSA) contractor, leaked classified documents to journalists, revealing extensive global surveillance programs. The leaked information exposed the NSA's mass data collection activities. Snowden claimed he acted in the public interest to expose government overreach and privacy violations. The incident sparked a global debate on surveillance, privacy rights, and government transparency.

CHELSEA MANNING (2010):

Chelsea Manning, a U.S. Army intelligence analyst, leaked classified military documents, including diplomatic cables and videos, to WikiLeaks. The leak, known as the Iraq War Logs, revealed information about military operations and diplomatic activities. Manning stated that she wanted to expose wrongdoing and facilitate public awareness. The leaks had diplomatic repercussions and raised questions about the handling of classified information.

HAROLD T. MARTIN III (2016):

Harold Martin, a contractor with the NSA, was arrested for stealing a massive amount of classified information over a period of 20 years. The stolen data included hacking tools and other sensitive materials. Martin's motivation remains unclear, but it was not believed to be politically or financially motivated. The incident highlighted the challenges of insider threats within intelligence agencies and raised concerns about the security of classified information.

TJX COMPANIES DATA BREACH (2005):

A group of hackers, led by Albert Gonzalez, exploited vulnerabilities in the wireless networks of TJX Companies (parent company of retailers like TJ Maxx) to steal credit card data and personal information of millions of customers. While not a traditional insider, the incident involved insider knowledge as the attackers used information from a previous job held by one of the hackers. The breach is one of the largest in history, resulting in significant financial losses and damage to the company's reputation.

UBS ROGUE TRADER (2011):

Kweku Adoboli, a trader at UBS, engaged in unauthorized trading activities that resulted in losses exceeding $2 billion. Adoboli concealed his trades and falsified records to hide the losses. Adoboli's actions were initially driven by a desire to boost his bonuses, but the trades eventually led to substantial losses. The incident raised questions about risk management practices and internal controls within financial institutions.

SOLARWINDS SUPPLY CHAIN ATTACK (2020):

A sophisticated cyberattack compromised the software supply chain of SolarWinds, a major IT management software provider. The attackers inserted a malicious update that led to the compromise of numerous government agencies and private organizations.: The attack was attributed to a nation-state actor, likely with espionage motives rather than financial gain. The incident highlighted the vulnerability of supply chains to sophisticated cyber threats and the potential for insider involvement in the software development process.

These examples underscore the diverse nature of insider threats, ranging from intentional data leaks for ideological reasons to unauthorized financial trading and cyberattacks facilitated by compromised insiders or supply chains. They emphasize the importance of robust security measures, continuous monitoring, and employee awareness to mitigate the risks associated with insider threats.

BEHAVIOURAL ANALYTICS AND ANOMALY DETECTION IN INSIDER THREAT DETECTION

Behavioral analytics involves the analysis of patterns and trends in user behavior over time. It establishes a baseline of normal behavior for individuals and identifies anomalies or deviations from that baseline.

Baseline Establishment: Behavioral analytics start by establishing a baseline of normal activities for each user. This baseline includes typical login times, access patterns, data usage, and other relevant behaviors.

Continuous Monitoring: Continuous monitoring allows the system to adapt to changes in user behavior over time. As users engage with systems, applications, and data, behavioral analytics platforms continuously update their understanding of what constitutes normal behavior.

User Profiling: User profiling involves creating detailed profiles for each user based on their historical behavior. These profiles help in distinguishing between regular activities and potentially malicious actions.

Contextual Analysis: Behavioral analytics consider the context of user actions. For example, logging in from a new location might not be suspicious if it aligns with a user's travel history, but it could be flagged if it deviates significantly.

Machine Learning Integration: Many behavioral analytics solutions leverage machine learning algorithms to enhance their accuracy in identifying patterns and anomalies. Machine learning models can adapt and improve over time as they encounter new data.

Alerting System: Behavioral analytics systems include alerting mechanisms to notify security teams when anomalous behavior is detected. Alerts are often accompanied by risk scores, indicating the level of suspicion associated with the observed behavior.

Use Case Examples: Behavioral analytics can be applied to various use cases, such as detecting unusual data access patterns, identifying privileged users engaging in high-risk activities, or flagging instances of data exfiltration.

ANOMALY DETECTION

Anomaly detection involves identifying patterns or behaviors that deviate significantly from the norm. It focuses on recognizing outliers in datasets or user behavior that may indicate potential security threats.

Statistical Models: Anomaly detection often relies on statistical models to establish what is considered normal. Deviations beyond a certain threshold are flagged as anomalies.

Unsupervised Learning: Anomaly detection is often implemented using unsupervised learning techniques, where the system learns from the data without specific labeled examples of anomalies.

Network Anomalies: In the context of insider threat detection, anomaly detection can be applied to network traffic. Unusual data transfer volumes, communication patterns, or connections may indicate potential insider threats.

Endpoint Anomalies: Anomaly detection can monitor endpoints for unusual activities, such as multiple failed login attempts, unauthorized software installations, or atypical data access.

Dynamic Thresholds: Dynamic thresholds in anomaly detection adjust over time based on evolving patterns. This adaptability is crucial for accommodating changes in user behavior and system dynamics.

BEHAVIORAL BIOMETRICS:

Anomaly detection can also incorporate behavioral biometrics, such as keystroke dynamics or mouse movement patterns, to create unique user profiles. Deviations from these profiles may trigger alerts.

USE CASE EXAMPLES

Anomaly detection can be applied to various use cases, including detecting unauthorized access to sensitive data, identifying suspicious login activities, or flagging abnormal changes in user permissions.

CHALLENGES AND CONSIDERATIONS

False Positives: Both behavioral analytics and anomaly detection may generate false positives. Balancing the sensitivity of detection with minimizing false alerts is a challenge.

Context Awareness: Understanding the context of user behavior is crucial. What may seem anomalous might be perfectly legitimate in certain situations.

Data Quality: The effectiveness of these methods relies on the quality and completeness of the data. Incomplete or inaccurate data may lead to misinterpretations.

Adaptability: Systems must be adaptable to changes in user behavior and system configurations. Regular updates to baselines and models are necessary.

MONITORING USER ACTIVITIES AND ACCESS FOR INSIDER THREAT DETECTION

Observing how individuals interact with systems, applications, and data can be leveraged to identify anomalous behaviors within an organization. By doing this, insider threats can be caught and dealt with in time.

MONITORING USER ACTIVITIES

User Logins and Logouts: Monitor the frequency, timing, and locations of user logins and logouts. Sudden changes in login patterns, especially outside regular working hours or from unusual locations, may indicate potential insider threats.

Authentication Attempts: Track authentication attempts, including successful and unsuccessful logins. Repeated failed login attempts or unauthorized access may signal malicious activities.

Data Access and Usage: Monitor which users access specific files, databases, or applications. Unusual data access patterns, especially accessing sensitive information without a legitimate reason, can be indicative of insider threats.

Privileged Access: Keep a close eye on users with privileged access rights. Monitoring their activities, especially outside their normal scope of responsibilities, is necessary for identifying potential misuse.

Network Traffic: Analyze network traffic associated with user activities. Unusual data transfer volumes, communication patterns, or connections may signify insider threats, particularly in the context of data exfiltration.

Endpoint Activities: Monitor activities on endpoints (computers, laptops, mobile devices). This includes software installations, changes in configurations, and interactions with removable media.

Email and Communication Monitoring: Keep an eye on email communications and other forms of digital communication. Unusual patterns, such as large data attachments or communication with external entities, may raise suspicion.

Application Usage: Track the usage of applications, especially those vital to business operations. Unusual or unauthorized application access may be indicative of insider threats.

MONITORING ACCESS

Access Permissions: Regularly review and audit access permissions for users. Ensure that individuals only have access to the resources necessary for their roles, and promptly revoke access for employees who no longer require it.

Role-Based Access Control (RBAC): Implement RBAC to assign access permissions based on job roles. This ensures that users have the minimum necessary access to perform their duties, reducing the risk of insider threats.

Access Reviews: Conduct regular access reviews to validate that users still require their assigned access rights. This process helps identify and rectify any discrepancies or unauthorized access.

Authentication Mechanisms: Enforce strong authentication mechanisms, such as multi-factor authentication (MFA), to add an additional layer of security. This helps prevent unauthorized access, especially in the event of compromised credentials.

Monitoring Privileged Access: Intensively monitor and restrict privileged access. Any changes or activities involving privileged accounts should be closely scrutinized to prevent misuse.

Data Encryption: Implement data encryption to protect sensitive information. This safeguards data even if unauthorized access occurs, making it more challenging for insiders to exploit data breaches.

BEHAVIORAL ANALYSIS OF ACCESS PATTERNS

Apply behavioral analysis to access patterns. Understand what constitutes normal access for each user and raise alerts for deviations, such as accessing data outside of regular job responsibilities.

REAL-TIME ALERTS

Configure real-time alerts for suspicious access activities. Automated alerting systems can notify security teams of potential insider threats, allowing for immediate investigation and response.

CHALLENGES AND CONSIDERATIONS

Balancing Privacy and Security: It's essential to strike a balance between monitoring for security purposes and respecting user privacy. Clearly communicate monitoring practices to employees and ensure compliance with privacy regulations.

False Positives: Monitoring may generate false positives. Fine-tuning monitoring systems and incorporating context-aware analysis helps reduce false alerts.

Insider Collaboration: Insiders may collaborate to avoid detection. Monitoring multiple users' activities and detecting unusual collaboration patterns is crucial.

Dynamic Environments: Environments evolve, and user roles change. Regularly update access permissions and adjust monitoring strategies to accommodate changes in the organization.

Integration with Other Security Measures: Monitoring should be integrated with other security measures, such as intrusion detection systems, security information and event management (SIEM) solutions, and endpoint protection, to provide a comprehensive security posture.

DATA ENCRYPTION AS A TOOL

Data encryption and classification are essential components of an organization's data protection strategy, especially in the context of mitigating insider threats. These measures help in safeguarding sensitive information, controlling access, and preventing unauthorized disclosure or misuse. Here's a detailed discussion of data encryption and classification in relation to insider threat prevention:

Data encryption is the process of converting plaintext data into ciphertext using cryptographic algorithms. This transformation ensures that even if unauthorized individuals gain access to the encrypted data, they cannot interpret it without the corresponding decryption key.

Role in Insider Threat Prevention

Encryption acts as a last line of defense, providing a layer of protection for data, especially when other security measures fail. In the event of unauthorized access, encrypted data remains indecipherable without the appropriate decryption key.

Types of Data Encryption

* *Symmetric Encryption:* Uses a single key for both encryption and decryption.

* *Asymmetric Encryption (Public Key Encryption):* Utilizes a pair of keys, one public and one private, for secure communication.

* *End-to-End Encryption:* Secures data in transit, preventing intermediaries, including insiders, from accessing the unencrypted data.

* *Endpoint Encryption:* Encrypting data on endpoints (devices like laptops and mobile devices) adds an extra layer of protection. If a device is lost or stolen, the encrypted data remains unreadable without the proper credentials.

* *Database Encryption:* Encrypting databases protect sensitive information stored within them. This is crucial for preventing unauthorized access to valuable data, even if an insider gains access to the database.

* *File and Folder Encryption*: Encrypting specific files or folders ensures that only authorized users with the correct decryption key can access sensitive documents.

Challenges

While encryption is a powerful tool, managing and securing encryption keys is very important. If encryption keys are compromised, it can lead to unauthorized access.

DATA CLASSIFICATION

Data classification involves categorizing data based on its sensitivity, importance, and confidentiality. This process helps organizations identify and prioritize the protection measures needed for different types of data.

ROLE IN INSIDER THREAT PREVENTION

Data classification assists in applying appropriate security controls to protect sensitive information. By categorizing data, organizations can focus on implementing stricter controls for high-risk data, making it more challenging for insiders to access or misuse.

TYPES OF DATA CLASSIFICATION

* *Confidentiality Levels:* Classifying data into categories like public, internal use, confidential, or restricted based on sensitivity.

* *Data Labels and Tags*: Assigning labels or tags to files and documents indicating their level of sensitivity.

* *Automated Classification:* Implementing automated tools to analyze content and assign classifications based on predefined policies.

* Access Controls: Data classification informs access controls. High-risk data, such as financial records or intellectual property, can be restricted to only those individuals who require access for their roles.

* *User Awareness:* Data classification enhances user awareness about the sensitivity of information. Employees are more likely to exercise caution when handling classified data, reducing the risk of unintentional insider threats.

* *Data Lifecycle Management:* Data classification facilitates effective data lifecycle management. Organizations can establish retention policies and guidelines for secure data disposal based on the classification of information.

CHALLENGES

Consistently applying and enforcing data classification policies can be challenging. Employees need to be educated on the importance of classification, and automated tools can assist in maintaining consistency.

INTEGRATION FOR INSIDER THREAT PREVENTION

1. *Combined Approach:* Combining data encryption and classification provides a robust defense against insider threats. Encrypting classified data adds an extra layer of protection, especially for the most sensitive information.

2. *Granular Controls:* Integrating both measures allows organizations to implement granular controls. For instance, highly classified documents may require stronger encryption and access restrictions.

3. *Dynamic Policies:* Dynamic policies that consider both data classification and encryption status can adapt to changes in the organization, ensuring ongoing protection against evolving insider threats.

4. *Monitoring and Auditing:* Regularly monitoring and auditing encrypted and classified data help organizations detect anomalous activities. Any attempt to access or modify sensitive information can trigger alerts for further investigation.

Data Loss Prevention Technologies

DLP technologies are security solutions designed to protect sensitive data by monitoring, detecting, and preventing unauthorized access or transmission. The primary objectives of DLP technologies include preventing data breaches, ensuring compliance with regulations, and safeguarding intellectual property.

Key Components of DLP Technologies:

1. *Content Discovery:* Identify and locate sensitive data throughout an organization, including data at rest, in transit, and in use.

2. *Policy Enforcement:* Implement and enforce policies that dictate how sensitive data should be handled, accessed, and transmitted.

3. **Monitoring and Analysis:** Continuously monitor data flows and user activities to identify patterns and behaviors indicative of potential data breaches.

4. *Encryption and Masking:* Apply encryption or data masking to protect sensitive information, rendering it unreadable or pseudonymous to unauthorized users.

5. *Endpoint Protection:* Implement controls on endpoints (computers, mobile devices) to prevent data leaks through removable storage, email, or other channels.

6. *Network-based Controls:* Monitor network traffic for data patterns that match predefined **policies, preventing unauthorized data transfers.**

7. *Cloud DLP:* Extend DLP capabilities to cloud environments, ensuring the protection of sensitive data stored or processed in cloud applications and services.

8. ***User and Entity Behavior Analytics (UEBA):*** Employ behavioral analytics to detect anomalous user activities that may indicate insider threats or compromised accounts.

9. ***Incident Response and Reporting:*** Provide tools for responding to incidents, investigating potential data breaches, and generating reports for compliance purposes.

Types of DLP Technologies

* *Network DLP:* Monitors and controls data in transit over the network, preventing unauthorized transfers or leaks.

* *Endpoint DLP:* Applies controls directly on endpoints, preventing data leaks through various channels, including USB drives, email, and printing.

* *Storage DLP:* Protects data at rest by monitoring and controlling access to stored data in databases, file servers, or data repositories.

* *Cloud DLP:* Extends DLP capabilities to cloud environments, ensuring the protection of sensitive data in cloud-based applications and services.

* *Email DLP:* Monitors and controls the content of emails to prevent the inadvertent or intentional transmission of sensitive information.

DLP Technologies Workflow

* *Content Discovery:* Identify sensitive data across the organization, including structured and unstructured data.

* *Policy Definition:* Create policies specifying how sensitive data should be handled, accessed, and transmitted.

* *Monitoring and Analysis:* Continuously monitor data flows, user activities, and network traffic for policy violations.

* *Incident Response:* Respond to and investigate incidents, take corrective actions, and generate reports for auditing and compliance.

CHALLENGES AND CONSIDERATIONS

1. *False Positives:* DLP solutions may generate false positives, flagging legitimate activities as policy violations. Fine-tuning is essential to minimize false alerts.

2. ***Integration with Existing Systems:*** Seamless integration with existing security infrastructure, such as SIEM (Security Information and Event Management) systems, is crucial for a holistic security posture.

3. ***User Education:*** Employee awareness and education are key components of DLP success. Users must understand policies and the importance of handling sensitive data responsibly.

4. ***Encryption Key Management:*** Proper management of encryption keys is very crucial to ensure that only authorized individuals can access encrypted data.

BENEFITS OF DLP TECHNOLOGIES

Some of the benefits of deploying DLP technologies include:

1. ***Data Protection:*** Prevents data breaches and protects sensitive information from unauthorized access or disclosure.

2. ***Compliance Assurance:*** Helps organizations meet regulatory requirements by enforcing data protection policies.

3. ***Intellectual Property Protection:*** Safeguards intellectual property by preventing unauthorized access or leaks.

4. ***Brand and Reputation Protection:*** Mitigates the risk of data breaches that could harm an organization's reputation and brand.

5. ***Incident Response and Investigation:*** Facilitates rapid incident response, investigation, and reporting in the event of a data breach.

DEVELOPING AN INCIDENT RESPONSE PLAN

So now, the deed has been done, your organization's data has been compromised, what next should you be doing to salvage the situation? This is where an Incident Response Plan comes in. An incident response plan outlines the procedures, roles, and actions to be taken in the event of a cybersecurity incident or data breach.

An effective incident response plan helps an organization detect, respond to, and recover from cybersecurity incidents in a systematic and organized manner. Below is a detailed outline of all you need to develop a plan for your organization.

1. *Establishing the Incident Response Team:*

    Roles and Responsibilities:

    Clearly define the roles and responsibilities of each team member. This may include incident coordinators, technical analysts, communication liaisons, legal representatives, and management.

    Communication Plan:

    Establish a communication plan outlining how the incident response team will communicate internally and externally during an incident. Define the chain of command and methods of communication.

2. *Identifying and Classifying Incidents:*

Define Incident Categories:

Categorize potential incidents based on their severity and impact. Common categories include malware infections, data breaches, denial-of-service attacks, and insider threats.

Incident Identification:

Establish methods for identifying and classifying incidents. This may involve implementing monitoring tools, conducting regular security assessments, and staying informed about emerging threats.

3. **Preparation and Planning:**

Risk Assessment:

Conduct a comprehensive risk assessment to identify and prioritize potential threats. This assessment helps in allocating resources appropriately.

Documentation:

Document most important assets, network configurations, and system details. Maintain an up-to-date inventory of hardware, software, and data assets.

Incident Response Policy:

Develop a formal incident response policy that outlines the organization's commitment to addressing and mitigating security incidents.

4. *Incident Detection and Reporting:*

Monitoring Systems:

Implement monitoring systems and intrusion detection tools to detect unusual or suspicious activities. Define thresholds for alerts and notifications.

User Reporting:

Establish a mechanism for users to report incidents or suspicious activities. Encourage a culture of reporting without fear of reprisal.

Automated Incident Reporting:

Implement automated incident reporting mechanisms to expedite the detection and response process.

5. *Response and Mitigation:*

Incident Triage:

Establish a process for triaging incidents based on their severity. This helps in prioritizing the response effort.

Containment Strategies:

Define strategies for containing incidents to prevent further damage. This may involve isolating affected systems, blocking malicious traffic, or shutting down compromised accounts.

Eradication:

Develop procedures for removing the root cause of the incident and ensuring that the organization is no longer vulnerable to the same type of attack.

Restoration:

Plan for restoring affected systems and services to normal operation. This may involve rebuilding systems from clean backups.

6. ***Communication and Reporting:***

Internal Communication:

Establish a clear and concise internal communication plan to keep all relevant stakeholders informed about the incident and response efforts.

External Communication:

Define procedures for communicating with external parties, such as regulatory bodies, law enforcement, customers, and the media, if necessary.

Post-Incident Reporting:

Document and analyze the incident response process after the incident is resolved. Identify lessons learned and areas for improvement.

7. ***Legal and Compliance Considerations:***

Legal Counsel Involvement:

Engage legal counsel early in the incident response process, especially for incidents involving data breaches or potential legal ramifications.

Regulatory Compliance:

Ensure that incident response procedures align with applicable regulatory requirements. Be prepared to report incidents to regulatory bodies as necessary.

8. *Training and Exercises:*

Employee Training:

Train employees on their roles and responsibilities during an incident. This includes awareness training to recognize and report potential incidents.

Tabletop Exercises:

Conduct regular tabletop exercises to simulate various incident scenarios. This helps in testing the effectiveness of the incident response plan and improving team coordination.

Post-Incident Review:

After each exercise or incident, conduct a thorough review to identify areas for improvement and update the incident response plan accordingly.

9. **Continuous Improvement:**

Metrics and Key Performance Indicators (KPIs): Establish metrics and KPIs to measure the effectiveness of the incident response plan. This may include incident detection time, response time, and containment success rates.

Feedback Loop: Implement a feedback loop to gather insights from incident response activities. Use this information to continuously refine and improve the incident response plan.

10. **Documentation and Retention:**

Incident Documentation: Document all aspects of each incident, including initial reports, response actions, and outcomes. This documentation is valuable for post-incident analysis and compliance purposes.

Retention Policy: Establish a data retention policy for incident-related records. Ensure compliance with legal and regulatory requirements regarding data retention.

11. *Integration with Business Continuity and Disaster Recovery:*

Alignment with BCDR Plans: Ensure that the incident response plan is integrated with the organization's Business Continuity and Disaster Recovery plans. This ensures a holistic approach to resilience.

Cross-Training: Cross-train incident response team members with those responsible for business continuity and disaster recovery. This enhances collaboration during tough incidents.

Developing an incident response plan is an ongoing process that requires collaboration, testing, and continuous improvement. By following these guidelines and customizing the plan to the organization's specific needs and risks, an incident response team can be better prepared to handle cybersecurity incidents effectively and minimize the impact on the organization's operations and reputation.

CONDUCTING FORENSIC INVESTIGATION

Forensic investigations aim to uncover evidence, analyze incidents, and provide insights into the nature of security breaches or cybercrimes. This sort of investigation requires a combination of technical expertise, legal understanding, and meticulous attention to detail. Collaboration with HR, Legal, and other relevant departments is essential to ensure a thorough and legally compliant investigation.

1.   ***Incident Identification and Triage:***

     Initial Assessment: Begin by identifying the incident that triggers the need for a forensic investigation. This could be anything from a suspected data breach to a malware infection.

     Incident Triage: Prioritize incidents based on their severity and impact. Determine the scope of the investigation and allocate resources accordingly.

2.   ***Preservation of Evidence:***

     Isolation: Isolate affected systems or devices to prevent further contamination or compromise. This is crucial for preserving the state of the environment at the time of the incident.

     Documentation: Document the state of the systems, networks, and relevant configurations before making any changes. This documentation serves as a baseline for comparison during the investigation.

     Chain of Custody: Establish and maintain a clear chain of custody for all evidence collected during the investigation. This ensures that the integrity of the evidence is maintained and can be verified in legal proceedings.

3.   ***Forensic Imaging:***

     Disk Imaging: Create forensic images of relevant storage devices, such as hard drives or memory. Forensic imaging preserves the original state of the data and allows investigators to work with a copy, minimizing the risk of altering the evidence.

     Memory Capture: Capture the volatile memory (RAM) of systems. This can provide insights into running processes, open network connections, and other volatile data that may be lost upon system shutdown.

4. *Analysis of Digital Evidence:*

File System Analysis: Examine file systems for signs of unauthorized access, file manipulation, or the presence of malicious files. Analyze file metadata, timestamps, and permissions.

Network Traffic Analysis: Analyze network logs and traffic to identify unusual or malicious activities. This includes examining firewall logs, intrusion detection system (IDS) alerts, and packet captures.

Malware Analysis: If malware is suspected, conduct detailed analysis to understand its behavior, capabilities, and potential impact. This may involve reverse engineering and sandboxing.

Registry Analysis: Analyze Windows Registry entries for evidence of malicious activities, persistence mechanisms, or changes made by attackers.

Email and Communication Analysis: Investigate email and communication logs for signs of phishing, unauthorized access, or data exfiltration.

5. *Timeline Reconstruction:*

Event Sequencing: Reconstruct a timeline of events leading up to, during, and after the incident. This helps investigators understand the sequence of actions and identify potential points of compromise.

Correlation of Artifacts: Correlate digital artifacts, such as log entries, timestamps, and file changes, to create a cohesive timeline. This aids in identifying the root cause and the extent of the incident.

6. ***Attribution and Identification:***

Attribution: If possible, attempt to attribute the incident to specific threat actors or groups. This requires a deep understanding of cyber threat intelligence and may involve collaboration with external security organizations.

User Identification: Identify the users involved in the incident, especially in cases of insider threats. This may require analyzing user logs, authentication records, and access permissions.

7. ***Documentation and Reporting:***

Forensic Report: Document all findings, methodologies, and evidence in a comprehensive forensic report. This report serves as a record for internal purposes and may be used in legal proceedings.

Legal Consultation: Engage legal counsel to ensure that the forensic report complies with legal requirements. Legal experts can provide guidance on the admissibility of forensic evidence in court.

8. ***Collaboration with Law Enforcement:***

Law Enforcement Involvement: In cases involving cybercrimes, collaborate with law enforcement agencies. Provide them with the necessary evidence and cooperate in the legal process.

Legal Assistance: Work closely with legal representatives to understand the legal implications of the investigation and to ensure that all actions are conducted in accordance with applicable laws.

9. *Post-Incident Review:*

Lessons Learned: Conduct a post-incident review to identify lessons learned and areas for improvement in the forensic investigation process. Update incident response plans based on these insights.

Continuous Improvement: Incorporate feedback from forensic investigations into ongoing improvement efforts. This may involve refining incident response procedures, enhancing training programs, or updating detection capabilities.

CHALLENGES AND TRENDS IN INSIDER THREAT MITIGATION

Insider threats, which can emanate from employees, contractors, or business associates with access to an organization's systems and data, continue to adapt and take on new forms. Understanding the evolving nature of insider threats is crucial for developing effective mitigation strategies. Here are key aspects of the evolving nature of insider threats:

1. **Diverse Motivations:**

Traditional Espionage to Financial Gain:

While traditional espionage remains a concern, the motivations for insider threats have diversified. Employees may now be driven by financial gain, whether through selling sensitive information to competitors or engaging in fraudulent activities.

Disgruntlement and Retaliation:

Disgruntled employees seeking revenge for perceived wrongs or grievances pose a significant threat. Insiders may sabotage systems, leak confidential information, or disrupt operations in acts of retaliation.

External Influences:

Insiders might be influenced by external factors, such as coercion by malicious actors or involvement in external criminal networks. This complexity adds a layer of difficulty in identifying and mitigating insider threats.

2. Technological Sophistication:

Exploiting Advanced Technologies:

Insiders are increasingly leveraging advanced technologies to carry out their activities. This includes using sophisticated malware, exploiting vulnerabilities, and utilizing encryption to hide their actions.

Insider Collaboration with External Threat Actors:

Insiders may collaborate with external threat actors, combining their internal knowledge with external technical expertise. This collaboration can result in more sophisticated and damaging attacks.

3. Remote Work Challenges:

Increased Attack Surface:

The shift to remote work has expanded the attack surface for insider threats. Remote access to sensitive systems and data introduces new challenges in monitoring and controlling insider activities.

Employee Burnout and Stress:

Remote work-related stress and burnout can contribute to insider threats. Employees feeling overwhelmed or disconnected may be more susceptible to engaging in risky behaviors that could compromise security.

4. **Data Exfiltration Techniques:**

Cloud-Based Storage and Collaboration Tools:

Insiders leverage cloud-based storage and collaboration tools for data exfiltration. This can include copying sensitive information to personal cloud accounts or sharing it through collaboration platforms.

Use of Encryption:

Insider threats increasingly involve the use of encryption to conceal their activities. This makes it challenging for traditional security measures to detect and prevent data exfiltration.

5. **Social Engineering and Phishing:**

Targeted Social Engineering:

Insider threats often involve targeted social engineering campaigns. Insiders may be manipulated through phishing or social engineering tactics to disclose credentials, provide access, or carry out malicious actions.

Manipulation of Trusted Relationships:

Insiders may exploit trusted relationships within the organization to carry out their activities. This can include manipulating colleagues, partners, or even senior management to gain access or trust.

6. **Supply Chain Risks:**

Third-Party and Supply Chain Connections:

Insiders can exploit supply chain relationships and third-party connections to infiltrate an organization's systems. This highlights the importance of assessing and managing risks beyond the organization's immediate boundaries.

Contractor and Vendor Risks:

Contractors and vendors with access to internal systems pose insider threat risks. Organizations need to extend their security measures to cover third-party entities with privileged access.

7. Insider Collusion:

Collaborative Insider Threats:

Insider threats may involve collusion among multiple insiders working together to achieve a common goal. This collaboration can be challenging to detect, especially when individuals coordinate their actions.

Silent Insider Threats:

Insiders may operate silently, without triggering traditional security alerts. This makes it difficult to detect their activities until the damage has been done.

8. Advanced Persistent Threats (APTs):

Long-Term, Covert Activities:

Insider threats are evolving towards more advanced persistent threats, involving long-term and covert activities. Insiders may patiently gather information and execute their actions over an extended period.

Customized Attack Strategies:

APT-style insider threats often involve customized attack strategies tailored to the organization's specific vulnerabilities and business processes.

Understanding the evolving nature of insider threats requires a proactive and adaptive security posture. Organizations should invest in technologies and practices that can identify anomalous behaviors, monitor remote work environments, and address the diverse motivations that drive insider threats.

EMERGING TECHNOLOGIES FOR INSIDER THREAT PREVENTION

Embracing emerging technologies is any organization's surest best in bolstering their defense against insider threats. However, it's crucial to approach their implementation with a comprehensive strategy that includes user education, policy development, and collaboration across departments.

USER AND ENTITY BEHAVIOR ANALYTICS (UEBA):

UEBA employs machine learning algorithms to analyze patterns of normal behavior among users and entities. It establishes a baseline and identifies anomalies that could indicate insider threats, such as unusual data access or login times.

BENEFITS:

UEBA enhances the ability to detect subtle deviations from normal behavior, providing a proactive approach to identifying insider threats. It helps organizations move beyond rule-based systems to dynamically adapt to evolving risks.

ENDPOINT DETECTION AND RESPONSE (EDR):

EDR solutions focus on monitoring and responding to activities on endpoints, such as computers and mobile devices. They detect malicious activities, including insider threats, by analyzing endpoint data and behavior.

BENEFITS:

EDR enhances visibility into endpoint activities, helping organizations swiftly identify and respond to potential insider threats. It provides real-time insights into user actions and facilitates rapid incident response.

ARTIFICIAL INTELLIGENCE (AI) AND MACHINE LEARNING (ML):

AI and ML technologies enable the automation of threat detection by learning from vast datasets. They can identify patterns, anomalies, and potential indicators of insider threats without relying on predefined rules.

BENEFITS:

AI and ML enhance the accuracy and speed of insider threat detection. These technologies can analyze massive datasets, identify subtle patterns, and adapt to evolving threats, improving the overall effectiveness of security measures.

DATA LOSS PREVENTION (DLP) SOLUTIONS:

DLP solutions monitor, detect, and prevent the unauthorized transmission of sensitive data. They use content inspection and contextual analysis to identify and block or encrypt sensitive information.

BENEFITS:

DLP solutions are crucial for preventing accidental or malicious data exfiltration by insiders. They provide granular control over data movement and help organizations maintain compliance with data protection regulations.

BLOCKCHAIN TECHNOLOGY:

Blockchain, with its decentralized and immutable ledger, can enhance the integrity of data and access logs. It provides a transparent and tamper-resistant record of user activities, making it more challenging for insiders to manipulate records.

BENEFITS:

Blockchain adds an additional layer of trust to activity logs and audit trails. It ensures the integrity of important data, making it a valuable technology for preventing insider threats and maintaining the integrity of digital records.

BEHAVIORAL ANALYTICS FOR NETWORK TRAFFIC:

Behavioral analytics applied to network traffic involves analyzing patterns in the flow of data to identify deviations from normal behavior. It helps detect anomalies that may indicate insider threats, such as unusual data transfers.

BENEFITS:

This technology provides insights into network-based activities, enabling the detection of potential insider threats based on deviations from established behavioral norms. It complements other security measures for a comprehensive approach.

ZERO TRUST SECURITY MODEL:

The Zero Trust model assumes that no user or system is inherently trusted, even if they are within the organizational network. It requires continuous verification of identity and authorization for all users and devices.

BENEFITS:

Zero Trust mitigates the risk of insider threats by implementing strict access controls and continuously verifying the legitimacy of user actions. It reduces the attack surface and enhances security in a parameter less environment.

Biometric Authentication and Multi-Factor Authentication (MFA):

Biometric authentication, such as fingerprint or facial recognition, adds an extra layer of identity verification. MFA requires users to provide multiple forms of identification, reducing the risk of unauthorized access.

Benefits:

These technologies enhance access control, making it more challenging for insiders to compromise user accounts. They add an additional layer of security beyond traditional username and password combinations.

Cloud Security Solutions:

As organizations increasingly rely on cloud services, specialized cloud security solutions offer protection against insider threats in cloud environments. These solutions monitor user activities, access, and data interactions.

Benefits:

Cloud security solutions provide visibility into user actions in cloud-based environments, helping organizations detect and respond to insider threats in the cloud. They address the unique challenges posed by the cloud's dynamic nature.

Threat Intelligence Platforms:

Threat intelligence platforms aggregate and analyze data from various sources to provide insights into emerging threats. They help organizations stay informed about potential insider threat vectors and tactics.

BENEFITS:

Threat intelligence platforms empower organizations to proactively address insider threats by staying ahead of emerging risks. By leveraging timely and relevant threat intelligence, organizations can strengthen their overall security.

CHAPTER 8

Leadership In GRC: The Roles Of Executives In Shaping Human Behaviour

"The role of executive leadership in GRC enablement of an organization is similar to that of a soccer team coach in a soccer game" (Vaidyula 2018). Leadership in GRC sets the tone for how everything else within the organization will work. Executives bear the responsibility of establishing a cultural tone that places emphasis on ethical conduct, strict compliance with regulations, and prudent risk management practices. The manifestation of these principles in executive behavior significantly shapes the ethical climate within the organization.

Impact on Employee Behavior

The influence of leadership on organizational behavior is profound. Employees tend to emulate the conduct of their leaders, and thus, when executives prioritize and exemplify GRC principles, a trickle-down effect is observed throughout the workforce. A positive GRC culture, fostered by leadership, instills a sense of responsibility and accountability among employees. This, in turn, reduces the likelihood of non-compliance, unethical behavior, and the occurrence of risks that may jeopardize the organization's integrity.

The Enron scandal of the early 2000s serves as a stark illustration of the catastrophic consequences that can arise in the absence of ethical leadership and a sound GRC culture. Conversely, companies such as Johnson & Johnson, with its renowned "Credo," exemplify the transformative impact of leadership fostering a values-driven culture.

STRATEGIC INTEGRATION OF GRC:

Effective leadership extends beyond setting cultural expectations to integrating GRC considerations seamlessly into the organization's overarching strategic planning. GRC, when approached strategically, becomes more than a mere compliance checklist; it becomes an intrinsic component of decision-making and strategy execution. Executives must comprehend the interconnected nature of governance, risk management, and compliance with the broader strategic objectives of the organization.

STRATEGIC ALIGNMENT:

A hallmark of effective leadership is the alignment of GRC objectives with the broader business goals of the organization. For instance, if a strategic objective involves expansion into new markets, executives must proactively assess and mitigate associated regulatory and operational risks. By ensuring GRC aligns with strategic goals, leaders position their organizations to leverage risk management as an enabler rather than a hindrance to business growth.

RISK-INFORMED DECISION MAKING:

Leaders play a pivotal role in championing a risk-informed approach to decision-making. This approach necessitates considering potential risks and compliance requirements when evaluating new initiatives, investments, or partnerships. Strategic integration ensures that GRC becomes an integral part of the decision-making process, contributing to a more resilient organization capable of navigating uncertainties and challenges.

In the aftermath of the 2008 financial crisis, the financial industry witnessed a paradigm shift in leadership approaches. Regulatory compliance and risk management became central to strategic decision-making within banks and financial institutions. This strategic integration was instrumental in rebuilding trust and ensuring long-term sustainability.

1. **Overview of the Role of Executives in Shaping Human Behavior**

Communication of GRC Expectations

Executives wield considerable influence in shaping human behavior by employing effective communication strategies to articulate GRC expectations clearly. This involves more than just disseminating policies; it entails ensuring that employees comprehend the rationale behind these policies. Communication channels may encompass town hall meetings, informative newsletters, interactive training sessions, and regular updates from leadership to maintain a continuous dialogue.

Alignment with Organizational Values

A key facet of executive leadership in shaping behavior lies in aligning GRC expectations with the organization's core values. When employees recognize that GRC is intricately linked to how the organization operates and upholds its values, they are more likely to internalize and adhere to these expectations. By emphasizing this alignment, executives instill a sense of purpose and commitment, reinforcing the idea that GRC is not merely a set of rules but an embodiment of the organization's ethos.

Reinforcement through Leadership Behavior

Executives contribute significantly to shaping human behavior by reinforcing GRC expectations through their own conduct. When leaders consistently adhere to policies and regulations, employees perceive the importance of compliance and ethical conduct Leadership behavior serves as a powerful model, influencing employees to adopt similar standards in their professional conduct and contributing to the cultivation of a GRC-conscious workforce.

2. Building a Risk-Aware Mindset

Leadership's Role in Risk Awareness

Executives play a pivotal role in fostering a risk-aware mindset throughout the organization. This involves creating a culture where employees are not only encouraged but feel a shared responsibility to identify, assess, and report risks, establishing a collective commitment to risk management. Leaders should underscore that risk awareness is not solely the province of a dedicated risk management team but a shared duty that permeates all levels and departments.

Integration with Performance Metrics:

Executives can further shape behavior by integrating risk awareness into performance metrics and evaluations. By weaving risk considerations into key performance indicators, leaders communicate that considering and managing risks is not only encouraged but is a fundamental expectation tied to high-performance standards. Recognizing and rewarding employees who demonstrate exceptional risk awareness and contribute to effective risk mitigation efforts further solidifies the importance of this mindset within the organizational culture.

Training and Education Initiatives:

Leadership should invest in ongoing training and educational initiatives aimed at enhancing employees' understanding of risk and compliance. This can encompass a variety of methods, including scenario-based training, workshops, and continuous learning programs. By making resources readily available and actively encouraging participation in educational opportunities, executives contribute to building a workforce that is not only informed about risk but also vigilant in identifying and addressing potential risks in their daily activities.

Embedding GRC in Strategic Planning:

Embedding Governance, Risk, and Compliance (GRC) in strategic planning involves aligning GRC objectives with the broader goals and mission of the organization. It requires a comprehensive understanding of how GRC contributes to, and is integrated into, the overall strategic direction of the organization. Executives play a pivotal role in ensuring that GRC objectives are strategically aligned. This involves active participation in the strategic planning process, advocating for the integration of GRC considerations at every stage. Executives should champion the idea that GRC is not a separate or standalone function but an integral part of achieving organizational objectives.

Risk-Informed Decision Making:

Embedding GRC in strategic planning necessitates making risk-informed decisions. It involves recognizing that risks and compliance considerations are not obstacles but integral factors that shape the decision-making process. Executives must encourage a proactive approach to identifying, assessing, and managing risks as part of the strategic decision-making framework. Executives need to advocate for a culture where risks are considered as inherent aspects of strategic decisions. This involves integrating risk assessments into the decision-making process, with leaders actively seeking input from risk management professionals. Leaders should set the expectation that risk assessments are not barriers but tools that enhance the organization's ability to navigate uncertainties and capitalize on opportunities.

3. Integration of GRC into Key Business Processes

Effective GRC integration requires that GRC considerations are woven into key business processes. This includes ensuring that GRC principles are inherent in areas such as project management, product development, and supply chain operations. GRC should not be a separate function but an integral aspect of how the business operates. Executives should work with functional leaders to embed GRC principles into their respective business processes. This might involve incorporating risk assessments, compliance checks, and ethical considerations into the workflow. Leadership should communicate the expectation that GRC is not an additional burden but a value-adding component that contributes to the efficiency and sustainability of business processes.

4. Alignment with Organizational Values and Culture

Embedding GRC in strategic planning necessitates a strong alignment with the organization's values and culture. GRC should reflect and reinforce the ethical principles and cultural norms that define the organization. This alignment ensures that GRC is not perceived as an external imposition but as an integral part of the organization's identity. Executives should actively participate in the development and reinforcement of the organizational values that underpin GRC. This involves ensuring that GRC objectives and practices are congruent with the stated values. Leaders play a crucial role in communicating that

GRC is not just about compliance but about upholding the ethical fabric and cultural identity of the organization.

5. **Continuous Monitoring and Adaptation**

Embedding GRC is not a one-time task; it requires continuous monitoring and adaptation to evolving risks and compliance requirements. Strategic planning should include mechanisms for ongoing assessment, monitoring, and adaptation of GRC strategies to address emerging challenges and changes in the business environment. Executives should establish a framework for continuous monitoring of GRC performance. This involves setting up key performance indicators (KPIs) that provide insights into the effectiveness of GRC strategies.

Leadership should actively participate in periodic reviews and adapt GRC strategies based on the changing risk landscape and regulatory environment. This demonstrates a commitment to staying ahead of challenges and maintaining the relevance of GRC in strategic planning.

6. **Communication of GRC Expectations in the Strategic Context**

To embed GRC effectively, executives must communicate GRC expectations within the strategic context. This involves clearly articulating how GRC aligns with and supports the achievement of strategic objectives. Communicating GRC expectations in this context ensures that employees understand the relevance and significance of GRC in achieving organizational goals. Executives should incorporate GRC messaging into overall communication about strategic priorities. This might include highlighting how adherence to GRC principles contributes to the long-term success of the organization. Leadership should actively participate in communication efforts, reinforcing the narrative that GRC is not a set of restrictive rules but a strategic imperative for sustainable growth.

7. Fostering a Risk-Aware Mindset

Fostering a risk-aware mindset begins with leadership actively cultivating awareness throughout the organization. Leaders play a pivotal role in instilling a sense of vigilance and understanding of potential risks among employees. Executives should communicate the importance of being vigilant and proactive in identifying potential risks. This involves emphasizing that risk awareness is a shared responsibility across all levels of the organization. Leadership should lead by example, showcasing a commitment to risk awareness in their decision-making processes and daily activities.

8. Integration of Risk Considerations into Decision Making

A risk-aware mindset entails considering potential risks as integral factors in decision-making processes. Leaders must advocate for and actively participate in the integration of risk considerations into strategic decisions, projects, and operational activities. Executives should champion a culture where risk assessments are a routine part of decision-making processes. This involves providing guidance on how to assess and mitigate risks associated with various initiatives. They should communicate that considering risks is not about avoiding all challenges but about making informed decisions that anticipate and manage potential negative impacts.

9. Promoting Open Communication Channels

Fostering a risk-aware mindset relies on open communication channels where employees feel comfortable reporting concerns and potential risks. Leadership plays a crucial role in creating an environment that encourages transparent communication.

Leadership should establish channels for employees to report risks, concerns, or observed non-compliance without fear of reprisal. This may involve setting up confidential reporting mechanisms or designated individuals for risk reporting. Executives should also actively communicate the value of open communication in identifying and addressing risks promptly, emphasizing that every employee has a role in risk identification.

10. Providing Ongoing Training and Education

To inspire a risk-aware mindset, continuous training and education are essential. Leadership should invest in programs that enhance employees' understanding of different types of risks, their implications, and the strategies for effective risk management.

Resources should be allocated for regular training sessions on risk awareness, ensuring that employees are well-informed about emerging risks and changes in the regulatory landscape. Leadership involvement in these training programs reinforces the organization's commitment to maintaining a knowledgeable and risk-aware workforce.

11. Setting Risk-Related Performance Metrics

Leadership can foster a risk-aware mindset by establishing performance metrics that include elements related to risk management. This sends a clear message that considering and managing risks is not only encouraged but is an integral part of achieving high performance. They should work with HR and relevant departments to integrate risk-related metrics into performance evaluations. This may include assessing an employee's ability to identify and mitigate risks in their role. They should also communicate that being risk-aware is a competency valued by the organization, linking it to career development and advancement opportunities.

12. Recognition and Rewards for Risk Awareness

Acknowledging and rewarding employees who demonstrate exceptional risk awareness reinforces the importance of cultivating a risk-aware mindset. Leadership should actively recognize and celebrate individuals or teams that contribute to effective risk identification and management. Recognition programs that highlight employees who consistently exhibit strong risk-aware behavior. This recognition may take the form of awards, public acknowledgment, or inclusion in success stories shared within the organization.

Leadership involvement in these recognition initiatives reinforces the organization's commitment to fostering a culture where risk awareness is valued and celebrated.

13. Incorporating Risk Scenarios in Training Simulations

Actively building a risk-aware mindset involves practical application. Leadership should advocate for the inclusion of risk scenarios in training simulations, providing employees with hands-on experience in identifying, assessing, and responding to potential risks. Executives should collaborate with training and development teams to design realistic simulations that expose employees to various risk scenarios relevant to their roles. Involvement in these simulations, perhaps through participation or support, underscores the organization's commitment to practical risk awareness and management.

14. Creating a Feedback Loop for Continuous Improvement

Leadership plays a key role in creating a feedback loop that encourages continuous improvement in risk awareness. This involves establishing mechanisms for gathering feedback on the effectiveness of risk management practices and incorporating lessons learned into future strategies. Executives should promote a culture where feedback on risk management practices is actively sought and valued. This may involve conducting post-implementation reviews after significant projects or initiatives to identify areas for improvement. Leadership should communicate the organization's commitment to learning from experiences and adapting strategies to enhance risk awareness continually.

RECOGNIZING AND ADDRESSING RISK TOLERANCE LEVELS

Risk tolerance refers to the amount of risk an organization is willing to accept or tolerate in pursuit of its objectives. Recognizing risk tolerance involves understanding the level of risk the organization considers acceptable in various aspects of its operations. Leadership should actively participate in defining risk tolerance levels, considering factors such as the organization's objectives, industry standards, regulatory requirements, and stakeholder expectations.

1. *Aligning Risk Tolerance with Objectives:* Effective risk management requires aligning risk tolerance with the organization's strategic objectives. Leadership must ensure that the level of risk accepted is congruent with the pursuit of organizational goals. Executives should engage in strategic discussions to ensure that risk tolerance aligns with the organization's mission, vision, and strategic plans.

2. ***Incorporating Stakeholder Perspectives:*** Recognizing risk tolerance involves considering the perspectives of various stakeholders, including customers, shareholders, employees, and regulatory bodies. Different stakeholders may have varying expectations and tolerances for risk. Opportunity should be created to facilitate dialogue with key stakeholders to understand their expectations regarding risk tolerance. This may involve regular communication, surveys, and feedback sessions.

3. ***Establishing Risk Appetite Statements:*** To formalize risk tolerance, organizations often create risk appetite statements. These statements articulate the acceptable level of risk and provide a framework for decision-making regarding risk-taking activities. Executives should lead the development of clear and concise risk appetite statements, collaborating with risk management professionals and relevant stakeholders.

4. ***Quantifying and Qualifying Risk Tolerance:*** Quantifying and qualifying risk tolerance involves translating abstract risk concepts into measurable terms. This can include defining thresholds for specific risk indicators and determining qualitative criteria for risk acceptance.

   Leadership should work with risk management teams to establish both quantitative and qualitative measures for risk tolerance. This may involve setting numerical thresholds for key risk indicators and defining scenarios that exceed acceptable risk levels.

5. ***Monitoring and Reviewing Risk Tolerance:*** Recognizing risk tolerance is a continuous process that requires continuous monitoring and periodic review. External and internal factors can influence an organization's risk landscape, necessitating adjustments to risk tolerance level. Organizations should establish mechanisms for regular monitoring of risk tolerance, integrating this into broader risk management processes. Leadership plays an important role in conducting periodic reviews to assess the relevance and effectiveness of existing risk tolerance levels, making adjustments as needed based on changing circumstances.

6. ***Educating and Communicating Risk Tolerance:*** Recognizing risk tolerance requires comprehensive education and communication efforts. Employees at all levels need to understand the organization's approach to risk and how their roles contribute to maintaining acceptable risk levels. In this case, leadership should lead initiatives to educate employees on the concept of risk tolerance, its relevance to the organization, and the role each individual plays in adhering to defined tolerances.

7. ***Adapting to Changing Circumstances:*** External and internal factors, such as changes in the business environment or emerging risks, may necessitate adjustments to risk tolerance levels. Recognizing and addressing these changes promptly is essential for effective risk management. Leadership should be proactive in adapting risk tolerance to changing circumstances. This involves staying informed about industry trends, regulatory developments, and emerging risks.

REGULATORY COMPLIANCE AND ACCOUNTABILITY

Regulatory compliance refers to an organization's adherence to laws, regulations, and standards relevant to its industry. These mandates are established by government authorities and industry bodies to ensure ethical conduct, consumer protection, data privacy, and the overall well-being of society. A comprehensive understanding of the regulatory landscape applicable to their industry is essential for leaders. This involves staying updated on existing regulations, anticipating changes, and assessing the potential impact on the organization.

1. ***Establishing a Compliance Framework:*** To ensure regulatory compliance, organizations need a structured compliance framework. This framework includes policies, processes, and controls designed to identify, assess, and mitigate compliance risks. The leadership of the organization should champion the development and implementation of a robust compliance framework. This involves collaborating with compliance officers, legal teams, and relevant stakeholders to establish policies and procedures that align with regulatory requirements.

2. ***Assigning Accountability for Compliance:*** Accountability is fundamental to regulatory compliance. Leadership needs to clearly define roles and responsibilities, designation. There should be collaboration department heads and compliance officers to assign accountability for compliance across various functions. This includes designating compliance officers, establishing reporting structures, and fostering a sense of ownership among employees.

3. ***Integrating Compliance into Business Processes:*** Compliance should be integrated into the fabric of business processes rather than treated as a separate function. Leadership needs to ensure that compliance considerations are woven into daily operations, decision-making, and strategic planning. Leadership should lead initiatives to integrate compliance into key business processes. This involves collaborating with department heads to embed compliance checks, risk assessments, and reporting mechanisms into routine activities.

4. ***Continuous Monitoring and Auditing:*** Continuous monitoring and auditing are essential for ensuring ongoing compliance. Leadership needs to establish mechanisms for regular assessments, internal audits, and reviews to identify and address any deviations from compliance requirements. Top level management should oversee the implementation of continuous monitoring programs and periodic audits. This involves working with internal audit teams, compliance officers, and external auditors to assess the effectiveness of compliance controls.

5. **Responding to Non-Compliance:** In the event of non-compliance, a swift and appropriate response is essential. Leadership should have procedures in place to investigate, address, and rectify non-compliance issues while implementing corrective actions to prevent recurrence. Executives should lead the response to non-compliance incidents, working with legal, compliance, and operational teams to conduct thorough investigations and implement corrective measures. They play a decisive role in communicating the organization's commitment to addressing non-compliance transparently and taking corrective actions to prevent future occurrences.

UNDERSTANDING THE REGULATORY LANDSCAPE

The regulatory landscape refers to the comprehensive framework of laws, regulations, and standards that govern an industry or business sector. It encompasses a wide range of legal requirements, from local and national laws to international standards, creating a complex environment that organizations must navigate.

Identification of Key Regulatory Bodies: Understanding the regulatory landscape requires identifying and comprehending the roles of key regulatory bodies that govern the industry. These bodies may include government agencies, industry-specific authorities, and international organizations setting standards relevant to the business. Organizations need to actively engage with and monitor the activities of key regulatory bodies. This involves establishing communication channels with regulatory authorities, participating in industry forums, and staying attuned to the regulatory agenda.

Assessment of Industry-Specific Regulations: Industries often have specific regulations tailored to their unique characteristics. Understanding the regulatory landscape requires a thorough assessment of industry-specific regulations that directly impact the organization's operations, products, and services. It is necessary to collaborate with legal and compliance teams to conduct regular assessments of industry-specific regulations. This involves identifying regulatory trends, emerging requirements, and any potential changes that might affect the organization. Leadership plays a key role in communicating the importance of industry-specific compliance to relevant stakeholders and aligning business strategies with regulatory expectations.

Global and Cross-Border Regulatory Considerations: For organizations with a global footprint, understanding the regulatory landscape extends to considering cross-border regulations. This includes compliance with international standards, data protection laws, and trade regulations that may impact the organization's cross-border activities. There is a need to take a proactive approach to understanding global and cross-border regulatory considerations. This involves collaborating with legal experts, trade associations, and international compliance teams.

Monitoring Regulatory Changes and Updates: The regulatory landscape is subject to continuous changes. Executives must establish mechanisms to monitor regulatory developments, updates, and amendments to ensure that the organization remains agile and responsive to evolving compliance requirements. A leader should oversee the implementation of robust systems for monitoring regulatory changes. This involves subscribing to regulatory updates, leveraging technology for real-time alerts, and allocating resources for regulatory intelligence.

Impact of Digital Transformation on Regulations: With the advent of digital transformation, regulations surrounding data privacy, cybersecurity, and technology usage have become prominent. Understanding the regulatory landscape requires executives to recognize the impact of digital advancements on compliance requirements. They should engage with technology and compliance teams to assess the implications of digital transformation on regulatory compliance. This involves understanding the intersection between technology trends, data protection laws, and industry-specific regulations.

IMPLEMENTING EFFECTIVE COMPLIANCE PROGRAMS

DEVELOPING AND COMMUNICATING COMPLIANCE POLICIES

1. **Risk Assessment and Policy Tailoring**

   Conduct a comprehensive risk assessment to identify potential compliance risks specific to the organization's industry, operations, and regulatory environment. Tailor compliance policies to address these risks, ensuring relevance and effectiveness.

   Implementation Steps:

   * Engage with legal and compliance experts to assess industry-specific risks.

   * Develop policies that align with identified risks, incorporating clear guidelines and expectations.

   Leadership Role:

   * Executives should champion the risk assessment process, emphasizing the importance of policies aligned with the organization's unique risk landscape.

   * Leadership plays a key role in communicating the strategic relevance of tailored policies to mitigate specific compliance risks.

2. **Clear and Accessible Policy Documentation:**

   Ensure that compliance policies are well-documented, easily accessible, and written in clear, understandable language. Establish a centralized repository or a digital platform for employees to access and reference policies.

   Implementation Steps:

   * Work with communication and IT teams to create a centralized policy repository.

* Regularly update policies to reflect changes in regulations or organizational processes.

Leadership Role:

* Executives should advocate for the creation of user-friendly, accessible policy documentation.

* Leadership plays a critical role in emphasizing the importance of clear communication and accessibility to ensure widespread understanding of policies.

3. **Employee Training on Policies:**

Conduct regular training sessions to educate employees on compliance policies. Ensure that employees understand the relevance of each policy, their role in adherence, and the consequences of non-compliance.

Implementation Steps:

* Develop engaging training materials, including e-learning modules, workshops, or seminars.

* Schedule periodic training sessions and integrate compliance education into onboarding processes.

Leadership Role:

* Executives should actively participate in and support employee training initiatives.

* Leadership plays a key role in reinforcing the message that compliance is a shared responsibility, starting with a thorough understanding of organizational policies.

4. **Communication of Policy Updates:**

Establish a robust communication plan for policy updates. Ensure that employees are promptly informed of any changes, and provide resources or training to help them adapt to the updated policies.

Implementation Steps:

* Use various communication channels, such as emails, intranet announcements, or company-wide meetings.

* Clarify the reasons behind policy updates and address common questions or concerns.

Leadership Role:

* Executives should endorse and actively participate in the communication of policy updates.

* Leadership plays a critical role in demonstrating the organization's commitment to keeping employees informed and engaged in compliance initiatives.

MONITORING AND ENSURING ADHERENCE TO COMPLIANCE REQUIREMENTS

1. **Regular Compliance Audits and Assessments:**

   Implement regular compliance audits and assessments to evaluate the effectiveness of policies and identify areas for improvement. Engage internal or external auditors to provide an objective evaluation.

   Implementation Steps:

   * Develop a schedule for periodic compliance audits.

   * Establish clear criteria for assessment and ensure audit findings are used for continuous improvement.

   Leadership Role:

   * Executives should actively participate in the oversight and support of compliance audits.

   * Leadership plays a key role in reinforcing the importance of audits as proactive measures for maintaining a robust compliance program.

2. **Establishing Reporting Channels:**

Create accessible and confidential channels for employees to report potential compliance violations. Encourage a culture of reporting and ensure that whistleblowers are protected from retaliation.

Implementation Steps:

* Develop a reporting mechanism, such as a hotline or an online platform.

* Clearly communicate the availability of reporting channels and emphasize the organization's commitment to non-retaliation.

Leadership Role:

* Executives should champion the establishment of reporting channels and support a culture that values transparency.

* Leadership plays a crucial role in fostering an environment where employees feel comfortable reporting concerns without fear of reprisal.

3. **Data Analytics for Monitoring:**

Leverage data analytics tools to monitor and analyze compliance-related data. This includes tracking key performance indicators (KPIs), monitoring employee behavior, and identifying trends that may indicate potential compliance issues.

Implementation Steps:

* Collaborate with IT and data analytics teams to develop relevant metrics.

* Implement regular data reviews to identify anomalies or patterns that may require further investigation.

Leadership Role:

* Executives should advocate for the use of data analytics as a proactive tool for compliance monitoring.

* Leadership plays a critical role in promoting a data-driven approach to identify and address compliance challenges promptly.

4. **Disciplinary Measures for Non-Compliance:**

Clearly define and communicate disciplinary measures for non-compliance. Ensure that these measures are consistently applied and aligned with the severity of the violation.

Implementation Steps:

* Work with HR and legal teams to establish a disciplinary framework.

* Communicate the consequences of non-compliance through training and policy documentation.

Leadership Role:

* Executives should support the consistent application of disciplinary measures.

* Leadership plays a key role in reinforcing the organization's commitment to a fair and transparent approach to addressing non-compliance.

The Role of Board and Governance Committee in Compliance Management

Setting The Tone At The Top

Boards and governance committees play a pivotal role in establishing the overall tone for compliance within an organization. Their commitment to ethical conduct and adherence to regulations sets the standard for the entire organization.

Implementation Steps:

* Clearly articulate the organization's commitment to compliance in the mission, vision, and values.

* Communicate the importance of compliance during board meetings and strategic planning sessions.

Leadership Role:

* Boards and governance committees should actively champion a culture of compliance at the highest level.

* Leadership plays a key role in ensuring that the commitment to compliance is reflected in the organization's guiding principles and strategic decisions.

Oversight of Compliance Programs:

Boards and governance committees are responsible for overseeing the effectiveness of the organization's compliance programs. This includes reviewing and approving compliance policies, monitoring adherence, and assessing the outcomes of compliance initiatives.

Implementation Steps:

* Establish a governance committee dedicated to compliance oversight.

* Regularly review and evaluate the organization's compliance policies and programs.

Leadership Role:

* Boards and governance committees should actively engage with compliance officers and executives to stay informed about the organization's compliance initiatives.

* Leadership plays a critical role in ensuring that compliance oversight is an integral part of board discussions and decision-making.

ALIGNING COMPLIANCE WITH STRATEGIC GOALS:

Boards and governance committees should ensure that compliance efforts align with the organization's strategic goals. This involves integrating compliance considerations into the strategic planning process and evaluating how compliance supports the achievement of broader objectives.

Implementation Steps:

* Include compliance updates and discussions in strategic planning sessions.

* Assess how compliance initiatives contribute to the organization's overall mission and goals.

Leadership Role:

* Boards and governance committees should actively advocate for the integration of compliance into strategic decision-making.

* Leadership plays a key role in communicating that compliance is not a standalone function but an integral component of the organization's long-term success.

RISK ASSESSMENT AND MITIGATION:

Boards and governance committees are responsible for overseeing risk management, including compliance risks. They should participate in regular risk assessments, ensuring that compliance risks are identified, evaluated, and mitigated effectively.

Implementation Steps:

* Collaborate with risk management teams to conduct comprehensive risk assessments.

* Review and approve risk mitigation strategies, particularly those related to compliance.

Leadership Role:

* Boards and governance committees should actively engage in discussions about compliance risks and mitigation strategies.

* Leadership plays a critical role in emphasizing the importance of proactive risk management to prevent compliance failures.

HIRING AND EVALUATING COMPLIANCE LEADERSHIP:

Boards and governance committees are responsible for hiring and evaluating the performance of compliance officers and leaders. Ensuring that the compliance leadership team possesses the necessary skills, experience, and ethical standards is crucial for effective compliance management.

Implementation Steps:

* Establish clear criteria for the selection of compliance officers.

* Regularly evaluate the performance of the compliance leadership team based on key performance indicators and ethical standards.

Leadership Role:

* Boards and governance committees should actively participate in the recruitment and evaluation of compliance leaders.

* Leadership plays a key role in ensuring that compliance leadership is held to the highest standards of competence and integrity.

COMMUNICATION WITH STAKEHOLDERS:

Boards and governance committees should communicate effectively with stakeholders, including shareholders, regulatory bodies, and the public. Transparent communication about the organization's commitment to compliance and the actions taken to ensure it is crucial for building trust.

Implementation Steps:

* Establish clear communication protocols for compliance-related matters.

* Regularly communicate compliance updates and achievements to stakeholders.

Leadership Role:

* Boards and governance committees should lead by example in transparent communication.

* Leadership plays a critical role in emphasizing the importance of building and maintaining trust through open and honest communication about the organization's commitment to compliance.

WHISTLEBLOWER PROTECTION AND REPORTING CHANNELS:

Boards and governance committees are responsible for ensuring the existence and effectiveness of whistleblower protection policies and reporting channels. These mechanisms encourage employees to report potential compliance violations without fear of retaliation.

Implementation Steps:

* Review and approve whistleblower protection policies.
* Monitor the effectiveness of reporting channels and address any shortcomings.

Leadership Role:

* Boards and governance committees should actively support the protection of whistleblowers.
* Leadership plays a key role in communicating that the organization values and protects employees who report compliance concerns.

LEGAL AND REGULATORY COMPLIANCE:

Boards and governance committees should ensure that the organization complies with all relevant laws and regulations. This involves staying informed about legal requirements, overseeing compliance initiatives, and addressing any legal issues that may arise.

Implementation Steps:

* Engage legal experts to provide regular updates on changes in relevant laws and regulations.
* Establish clear procedures for addressing legal and regulatory compliance challenges.

Leadership Role:

* Boards and governance committees should actively participate in discussions about legal and regulatory compliance.

* Leadership plays a critical role in communicating the organization's commitment to operating within the bounds of the law and upholding ethical standards.

EXAMINING INSTANCES OF EFFECTIVE EXECUTIVE LEADERSHIP IN GOVERNANCE, RISK, AND COMPLIANCE (GRC):

1. **Proactive Risk Management by Marriott International:**

   Marriott International, under the leadership of its executives, has demonstrated proactive risk management in the hospitality industry. The company faced a significant data breach in 2018, impacting millions of customers. In response, Marriott executives took swift action to investigate, address the issue, and implement enhanced cybersecurity measures. Executives led a thorough investigation into the breach, collaborating with cybersecurity experts to understand the extent of the incident. Marriott's leadership prioritized transparent communication with affected customers, regulatory authorities, and the public, showcasing accountability and commitment to addressing the issue.

   The proactive approach taken by Marriott's executives helped rebuild trust with customers, demonstrating that effective executive leadership in GRC involves swift action, transparency, and a commitment to continuous improvement.

2. **Compliance Excellence at Johnson & Johnson:**

   Johnson & Johnson, a multinational pharmaceutical and consumer goods company, has been recognized for its commitment to compliance and ethical practices. Executives at Johnson & Johnson prioritize compliance with regulatory requirements and ethical conduct in all aspects of the business. Executives at Johnson & Johnson have established and maintained a comprehensive compliance program that includes regular training, clear communication of policies, and continuous monitoring of compliance metrics. The leadership at Johnson & Johnson prioritized transparent reporting on compliance matters, ensuring that stakeholders are well-informed about the company's commitment to ethical practices.

   Johnson & Johnson's commitment to compliance has contributed to its positive reputation and sustained success. Effective executive leadership in GRC, in this case, involves setting high ethical standards, implementing a strong compliance framework, and fostering a culture of integrity throughout the organization.

3. **Strategic Risk Management at Microsoft:**

   Microsoft, led by its executives, has demonstrated effective strategic risk management in the ever-evolving technology landscape. Executives at Microsoft recognize the importance of anticipating and addressing risks associated with rapidly changing technologies, cybersecurity threats, and global regulatory environments. Microsoft's executives conduct ongoing risk assessments that consider emerging technologies, geopolitical changes, and evolving cyber threats. This proactive approach allows the company to stay ahead of potential risks.

Recognizing the increasing importance of cybersecurity, Microsoft's leadership has invested heavily in cybersecurity measures and threat intelligence, showcasing a commitment to protecting customer data and maintaining trust.

Microsoft's strategic risk management, led by executives, has positioned the company as a leader in the technology industry. Effective executive leadership in GRC involves a forward-looking approach to risk, strategic investment in mitigating threats, and a commitment to maintaining the highest standards of security.

4. **Ethical Leadership at Patagonia:**

Patagonia, a company known for its commitment to environmental and social responsibility, exemplifies ethical leadership in the realm of GRC. Executives at Patagonia have integrated ethical considerations into the company's core values and business practices. Patagonia's executives have championed sustainable and environmentally friendly business practices. This includes responsible sourcing, reducing the company's environmental footprint, and advocating for environmental causes.

They have prioritized social responsibility, including fair labor practices and community engagement. This commitment extends to supply chain transparency and ethical treatment of workers.

Patagonia's ethical leadership has not only contributed to the company's success but has also positioned it as a leader in corporate social responsibility. Effective executive leadership in GRC, in this instance, involves aligning business practices with ethical values, contributing positively to society, and fostering a culture of responsibility.

5. **Comprehensive Compliance Framework at Siemens:**

Siemens, a global industrial conglomerate, faced a high-profile corruption scandal in the early 2000s. In response, the company's executives implemented a comprehensive compliance framework to address ethical lapses and rebuild trust. Their executives led a significant overhaul of the company's compliance program, emphasizing a zero-tolerance approach to corruption and bribery. The executives also actively communicated their commitment to ethical business practices, holding themselves and employees accountable for compliance with anti-corruption laws.

Siemens' commitment to a robust compliance framework has resulted in a cultural shift within the organization, emphasizing ethical conduct. Effective executive leadership in GRC, in this case, involves acknowledging past mistakes, implementing corrective measures, and fostering a culture of integrity and compliance.

CHAPTER 9

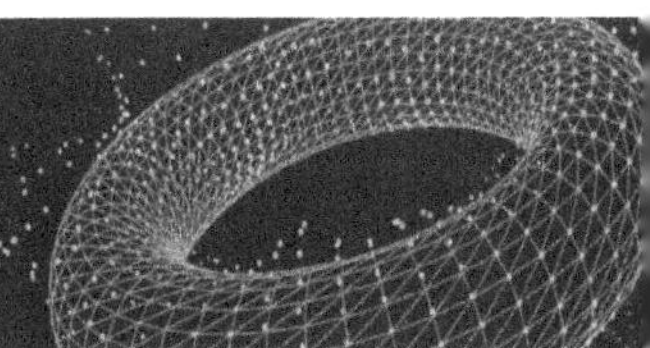

Whistleblowing and Ethics in GRC: Navigating the Thin Line of Reporting and Retribution

The Purpose of Whistleblowing

Whistleblowing refers to the act of an individual, typically an employee, disclosing information about wrongdoing or unethical behavior within an organization. The disclosure may involve reporting activities such as fraud, corruption, safety violations, discrimination, or other forms of misconduct.

Miceli et al. (2009) argued that whistle-blowing behavior does not occur often compared to other behaviors. At the same time, it is difficult to observe because most of them are conducted through confidential hot-lines or anonymous letters.

KEY COMPONENTS OF WHISTLEBLOWING:

A. Acting in the Public Interest:

1. Whistleblowers act in the interest of public welfare by exposing activities that may harm individuals, communities, or the broader society.

2. Their disclosures aim to address issues affecting stakeholders beyond the organization itself.

B. Protection Mechanisms:

1. Legal protections and safeguards are crucial for whistleblowers to encourage reporting without fear of retaliation.

2. Whistleblower protection laws vary by jurisdiction but commonly include provisions to shield individuals from adverse actions.

C. Internal vs. External Reporting:

1. Whistleblowers may choose to report concerns internally through established channels or externally to regulatory bodies, law enforcement, or the media.

2. The decision often depends on the organization's responsiveness to internal reporting and the severity of the wrongdoing.

MAINTAINING ORGANIZATIONAL INTEGRITY

Whistleblowing reinforces the importance of ethical conduct and adherence to organizational values. It signals a commitment to maintaining integrity, which is essential for building trust among employees, customers, and stakeholders.

The act of whistleblowing serves as a proactive mechanism for preventing and addressing wrongdoing before it escalates. Timely reporting allows organizations to investigate and rectify issues, minimizing potential harm.

Ensuring Transparency

Open Communication: Whistleblowing fosters open communication within an organization. Transparency in addressing concerns demonstrates a commitment to accountability and a willingness to confront challenges.

Building Trust: Transparent handling of whistleblowing cases builds trust among employees, investors, and the public. Trust is vital for maintaining a positive organizational reputation and attracting top talent.

Accountability and Governance:

Whistleblowing is an integral part of effective corporate governance. It ensures that there are checks and balances in place, holding individuals and the organization accountable for their actions. Trevino et al. (2006) pointed out that whistle-blowing behavior is a high-ethical organizational behavior.

It also contributes to legal compliance by addressing activities that may violate laws and regulations. Organizations that actively address reported concerns demonstrate a commitment to upholding legal standards.

CHALLENGES AND CONSIDERATIONS:

A. Fear of Retaliation:

1. Whistleblowers often face the risk of retaliation, including harassment or job loss.

2. Organizations must actively work to eliminate the fear of reprisal and create a supportive environment for reporting.

B. Organizational Culture:

1. The effectiveness of whistleblowing depends on the organization's culture.

2. Cultures that encourage ethical behavior and accountability are more likely to have robust whistleblowing mechanisms.

Summarizing the Role of Whistleblowing: Whistleblowing is a crucial mechanism for maintaining organizational integrity, transparency, and accountability. Its effectiveness depends on a combination of legal protections, ethical culture, and a commitment to addressing reported concerns.

CALL TO ACTION

A. Encouraging Whistleblowing Best Practices:

1. Organizations should actively promote and support whistleblowing best practices.

2. Encouraging employees to report concerns and ensuring fair treatment for whistleblowers contributes to a healthy and responsible organizational environment.

3. Whistleblowers often find themselves caught in a complex ethical dilemma when facing the decision to report misconduct within an organization. This

ethical challenge arises from conflicting values and obligations, and understanding the nature of this dilemma is crucial for appreciating the courage and moral fortitude required of whistleblowers. Let's take a look at an exploration of the ethical dilemmas faced by whistleblowers:

1. ***Loyalty vs. Integrity:***

Whistleblowers often feel a sense of loyalty to their organization, colleagues, or superiors. Reporting misconduct may be perceived as a breach of this loyalty. Balancing loyalty with the ethical obligation to uphold integrity and prevent harm poses a significant challenge.

2. ***Consequences of Speaking Out:***

They face the potential consequences of retaliation, ranging from professional isolation to job loss. This fear of reprisal creates a moral dilemma about whether to prioritize personal well-being or the greater good. Evaluating the ethical responsibility to expose wrongdoing against the personal and professional risks associated with speaking out.

3. ***Uncertain Outcomes:***

Whistleblowers may grapple with uncertainty regarding the outcomes of their actions. They may question whether their disclosure will lead to positive change or if it will result in unintended negative consequences. Weighing the potential benefits of exposing misconduct against the potential harm or lack of impact requires a careful ethical assessment.

4. ***Protecting Colleagues vs. Exposing Wrongdoing:***

Some whistleblowers may have close relationships with colleagues involved in the misconduct. Balancing the desire to protect colleagues with the duty to expose wrongdoing creates an ethical tension. Determining the ethical responsibility to the broader community, stakeholders, and the organization as a whole, while considering the impact on personal relationships.

5. ***Navigating Organizational Loyalty:***

Oftentimes, Whistleblowers may struggle with conflicting loyalties to the organization's success and reputation. Reporting misconduct could potentially harm the organization, leading to ethical tensions. Balancing loyalty to the organization with the greater ethical imperative of preventing harm, upholding values, and ensuring accountability.

6. ***Legal and Ethical Obligations:***

Whistleblowers may face situations where legal obligations and ethical responsibilities appear to be at odds. Deciding whether to comply with legal mandates or prioritize broader ethical considerations presents a dilemma. Navigating the interplay between legal requirements and moral duties, and deciding when one must take precedence over the other.

7. ***Internal Reporting vs. External Disclosure:***

There are occasions where whistleblowers often grapple with whether to report misconduct internally through organizational channels or externally to regulatory bodies or the media. This decision involves considerations of trust, effectiveness, and potential consequences. Evaluating the ethical implications of choosing the most effective reporting method while considering the impact on the organization and its stakeholders.

POTENTIAL RISKS OF RETALIATION: IMPACT ON INDIVIDUALS AND ORGANIZATIONS

The potential risks of retaliation against whistleblowers can have significant and far-reaching consequences, affecting both individuals and organizations. Understanding these risks is essential for creating a supportive environment that encourages ethical reporting. Here's a detailed exploration of the potential risks and their impact:

1. **Professional Repercussions:**

   Risk: Whistleblowers may face negative consequences in their professional lives, including demotion, denial of promotions, or being marginalized within the workplace.

   Impact: Fear of professional repercussions can deter individuals from reporting misconduct, compromising the organization's ability to address issues promptly.

2. **Job Loss:**

   Risk: Retaliation may escalate to the point of termination or forced resignation.

   Impact: Job loss not only affects the whistleblower's livelihood but also sends a chilling message to other employees, creating a culture of fear and discouraging reporting.

3. **Isolation and Hostility:**

   Risk: Whistleblowers may experience social isolation, hostility from colleagues, or exclusion from work-related activities.

   Impact: This hostile work environment can lead to stress, anxiety, and a decline in overall well-being, affecting both personal and professional life.

4. **Psychological and Emotional Toll:**

Risk: Retaliation can take a toll on the mental health of whistleblowers, leading to stress, anxiety, depression, or other psychological challenges.

Impact: The emotional burden may impact job performance, relationships, and overall quality of life.

5. **Financial Consequences:**

Risk: Whistleblowers may face financial repercussions, including loss of income, legal expenses, or challenges in finding future employment.

Impact: Financial strain adds an additional layer of stress, potentially deterring others from coming forward with important information.

6. **Damage to Reputation:**

Risk: Retaliation can involve efforts to tarnish the whistleblower's reputation within the organization or industry.

Impact: A damaged reputation can have long-term consequences, affecting career opportunities and personal relationships.

7. **Legal Battles:**

Risk: Whistleblowers may become entangled in legal battles, facing lawsuits or counterclaims from the organization.

Impact: Legal proceedings can be emotionally draining, financially burdensome, and may deter others from reporting misconduct due to the perceived risks.

8. **Impact on Organizational Culture:**

   Risk: A culture that tolerates or encourages retaliation can lead to decreased trust, low morale, and a reluctance among employees to report issues.

   Impact: A toxic work environment hampers organizational effectiveness, innovation, and the ability to address systemic problems.

9. **Regulatory Scrutiny:**

   Risk: Organizations engaging in retaliation may attract regulatory scrutiny and legal consequences.

   Impact: Legal penalties and reputational damage can harm the organization's standing and financial stability.

10. **Undermining Ethical Culture:**

    Risk: Retaliation sends a clear message that ethical behavior is not valued, undermining efforts to cultivate an ethical organizational culture.

    Impact: Employees may become disillusioned, leading to decreased commitment to organizational values and ethical principles.

THE EXISTENCE AND SIGNIFICANCE OF WHISTLEBLOWER PROTECTION LAWS

Whistleblower protection laws exist to safeguard individuals who, in good faith, report suspected misconduct, violations of laws, or unethical practices within organizations. The significance of these laws lies in providing legal mechanisms to shield whistleblowers from retaliation and encourage a culture of accountability. Here's an exploration of the existence and importance of whistleblower protection laws:

1. **Existence of Whistleblower Protection Laws:**

   International and National Legislation: Many countries have enacted laws at the national level to protect whistleblowers. Additionally, there are international initiatives and agreements addressing whistleblower protection.

   Industry-Specific Legislation: Some industries have specific laws to protect whistleblowers, recognizing the unique challenges they may face in certain sectors.

2. **Significance of Whistleblower Protection Laws:**

   Encouraging Reporting: Whistleblower protection laws play a crucial role in encouraging individuals to come forward with information about wrongdoing. Without legal safeguards, fear of retaliation could deter potential whistleblowers, hindering the exposure of misconduct.

   Promoting Accountability: Protection laws reinforce the importance of accountability within organizations and society. When individuals feel secure in reporting misconduct, organizations are better equipped to address issues, preventing potential harm and promoting ethical conduct.

   Fostering Transparency: Whistleblower protection laws contribute to organizational transparency by ensuring that information about misconduct is not suppressed. Transparent reporting mechanisms build trust among stakeholders and enhance the overall integrity of organizations.

   Preventing Retaliation: Protection laws explicitly prohibit retaliation against whistleblowers. Knowing they are legally shielded from adverse actions, whistleblowers are more likely to come forward without fear of losing their jobs or facing other negative consequences.

Legal Recourse for Whistleblowers: Whistleblower protection laws provide legal recourse for individuals who face retaliation. This legal protection empowers whistleblowers to seek remedies for damages and ensures accountability on the part of organizations engaging in retaliatory actions.

Facilitating Investigations: Whistleblower reports often trigger investigations into alleged misconduct. Protection laws facilitate thorough and unbiased investigations by providing a secure avenue for reporting and ensuring the confidentiality of whistleblowers.

Cultural Shift Towards Ethical Conduct: Whistleblower protection laws contribute to a cultural shift by promoting ethical behavior. When individuals see that reporting, misconduct is not only encouraged but also legally protected, it reinforces the value of ethical conduct within organizations.

KEY COMPONENTS OF WHISTLEBLOWER PROTECTION LAWS:

* Confidentiality and Anonymity: Laws often include provisions to protect the confidentiality and anonymity of whistleblowers.

* Non-Retaliation Provisions: Whistleblower protection laws explicitly prohibit retaliation against individuals who report misconduct.

* Legal Remedies: Laws provide legal remedies for whistleblowers who face retaliation, including compensation for damages and reinstatement to their positions.

CHALLENGES AND EVOLVING LEGISLATION:

* Global Variances: Whistleblower protection laws vary globally, and some regions may have stronger or weaker protections.

* Evolving Legislation: Legislators continue to refine and strengthen whistleblower protection laws to address emerging challenges and ensure their effectiveness.

HOW ORGANIZATIONS SHOULD RESPOND TO WHISTLEBLOWER REPORTS AND RETALIATION

Organizations should approach whistleblower reports and instances of retaliation with a well-defined and ethical response strategy. A robust response is crucial for fostering a culture of transparency, accountability, and fairness. Here's an examination of how organizations should respond to whistleblower reports and incidents of retaliation:

1. *Establish Clear Reporting Mechanisms:*

   Whistleblower Hotlines and Channels: Organizations should have clear and easily accessible reporting mechanisms, such as hotlines, dedicated email addresses, or web portals. These channels should be widely communicated to employees, stakeholders, and, where applicable, external parties.

2. *2. Confidentiality and Anonymity:*

   Preserve Whistleblower Confidentiality: Organizations must prioritize the confidentiality of whistleblower identities. Confidential reporting encourages individuals to come forward without fear of retaliation.

3. *Prompt and Thorough Investigations:*

Appoint a Dedicated Investigation Team: Designate a specialized team or individual responsible for thoroughly investigating whistleblower reports. Ensure the team has the necessary expertise and independence to conduct unbiased investigations.

4. *Non-Retaliation Commitment:*

Explicit Non-Retaliation Policy: Organizations should have a well-defined non-retaliation policy, emphasizing that retaliation against whistleblowers is strictly prohibited. Communicate this policy clearly to all employees, and include it in relevant documentation such as employee handbooks.

5. *Legal Compliance:*

Ensure Compliance with Whistleblower Protection Laws: Organizations should be well-versed in local and international whistleblower protection laws and ensure strict compliance. Adhering to legal requirements protects both the organization and the whistleblower.

6. *Communication and Support:*

Open and Supportive Communication: Communicate openly with the whistleblower throughout the investigation process. Provide emotional and legal support, demonstrating the organization's commitment to fairness and justice.

7. *Corrective Actions and Accountability:*

Addressing Substantiated Concerns: If the investigation substantiates the whistleblower's concerns, take swift and appropriate corrective actions. Hold accountable those responsible for misconduct, ensuring a fair and just resolution.

8. *Periodic Reporting to Leadership and Boards:*

    Reporting to Leadership and Boards: Periodically update senior leadership and, where applicable, boards of directors on the status of whistleblower investigations. Ensure transparency and accountability at the highest organizational levels.

9. *Learning and Improvement:*

    Continuous Improvement: Learn from each whistleblower case to enhance internal controls, policies, and procedures. Use insights gained to improve the organization's response to future reports.

10. *Support for Whistleblowers Post-Investigation:*

    Post-Investigation Support: Provide ongoing support to whistleblowers even after the investigation is concluded. Monitor for any signs of retaliation and address them promptly.

11. *Legal Protections:*

    Legal Protections for Whistleblowers: Organizations should respect and uphold legal protections afforded to whistleblowers. Understand the legal implications of whistleblower cases and act in accordance with applicable laws.

THE FUTURE OF WHISTLEBLOWING: TECHNOLOGY AND TRENDS

Technological advances, particularly the development of secure reporting platforms, have a profound impact on the future of whistleblowing. These advancements enhance the effectiveness, security, and accessibility of whistleblower reporting mechanisms, fostering a culture of transparency and accountability. Here's an exploration of how technological advances are shaping the future of whistleblowing:

1. ***Secure and Anonymous Reporting Platforms:***

    Encrypted Communication: Technological advances enable the use of end-to-end encryption, ensuring the confidentiality of whistleblower communications. Whistleblowers can report concerns without fear of interception or identification.

    Anonymous Reporting Options: Secure platforms allow whistleblowers to submit reports anonymously, providing an additional layer of protection. Anonymity encourages individuals to come forward with sensitive information, knowing their identity is safeguarded.

2. ***User-Friendly Interfaces:***

    Intuitive Design: Advanced reporting platforms prioritize user-friendly interfaces, making it easier for individuals to submit reports. Accessibility and ease of use enhance the likelihood of reporting and contribute to a positive user experience.

    Multichannel Accessibility: Whistleblowers can access reporting platforms through various channels, including web portals, mobile applications, and dedicated email addresses. Multichannel accessibility ensures that individuals can report misconduct using their preferred method.

3. ***Artificial Intelligence (AI) and Machine Learning (ML):***

    Automated Triage and Categorization: AI and ML technologies can be employed to automate the initial triage and categorization of whistleblower reports. Automated processes help prioritize urgent cases and streamline the investigative workflow.

    Pattern Recognition: AI algorithms can identify patterns in reporting data, helping organizations detect systemic issues and trends. Pattern recognition enhances the organization's ability to proactively address potential misconduct.

4. *Enhanced Security Measures:*

Blockchain Technology: Blockchain can be employed to enhance the security and immutability of whistleblower reports. This technology ensures that once a report is submitted, its contents remain unchanged and verifiable.

Access Controls and Auditing: Technological advancements enable the implementation of robust access controls and auditing features. Organizations can track who accesses whistleblower reports, ensuring accountability and preventing unauthorized disclosures.

5. *Integration with Case Management Systems:*

Streamlined Investigations: Reporting platforms can integrate seamlessly with case management systems, streamlining the investigative process. Integration ensures that reported concerns are efficiently managed and addressed.

Data Consolidation and Analysis: Integrated systems facilitate the consolidation and analysis of data from various sources. Data-driven insights contribute to a more comprehensive understanding of organizational risks and potential misconduct.

6. *Real-Time Reporting and Monitoring:*

Instantaneous Reporting: Advanced reporting platforms enable real-time reporting, allowing whistleblowers to submit concerns as soon as they arise. Real-time reporting enhances the organization's ability to respond promptly to emerging issues.

Continuous Monitoring: Organizations can implement continuous monitoring features to track the status of whistleblower reports in real time. This ensures that investigative processes are efficient, and stakeholders are kept informed.

7. *Machine Translation for Global Reporting:*

Multilingual Support: Technological advances in machine translation support multilingual reporting. This is especially crucial for global organizations, ensuring that language barriers do not hinder reporting from diverse regions.

Cultural Sensitivity: AI-powered language processing can assist in identifying and addressing cultural nuances in reported concerns. Cultural sensitivity enhances the organization's ability to respond appropriately to diverse whistleblower reports.

Technological advances, particularly in secure reporting platforms, are transforming the landscape of whistleblowing. These innovations not only enhance the security and confidentiality of reporting but also streamline the investigative process, provide real-time insights, and contribute to a culture of accountability. As organizations continue to leverage these advancements, the future of whistleblowing is characterized by increased accessibility, efficiency, and the ability to proactively address misconduct.

THE NEED FOR INTERNATIONAL COLLABORATION ON WHISTLEBLOWER PROTECTION

International collaboration on whistleblower protection is imperative to address the global nature of many issues that whistleblowers may expose and to ensure consistent and effective protection for individuals who come forward with information about wrongdoing. Here are several key reasons highlighting the need for international collaboration on whistleblower protection:

1. ***Cross-Border Issues:***

    Global Reach of Misconduct: Many instances of misconduct, such as corruption, fraud, or environmental violations, transcend national borders. International collaboration is essential to address issues that have cross-border implications and impact multiple jurisdictions.

    Whistleblowers in Different Countries: Whistleblowers may reside in one country while reporting misconduct that occurs in another. Collaborative efforts are needed to ensure that these individuals receive adequate protection, regardless of their location.

2. ***Consistency in Protection:***

    Harmonizing Standards: Different countries have varying legal frameworks and standards for whistleblower protection. Collaboration helps harmonize these standards, ensuring that whistleblowers are consistently protected regardless of where they are located or where the reported misconduct occurred.

    Addressing Legal Gaps: Some jurisdictions may lack comprehensive whistleblower protection laws, leaving individuals vulnerable to retaliation. International collaboration can assist in addressing these gaps and advocating for stronger legal safeguards.

3. ***Global Challenges:***

    Global challenges such as climate change, corruption, and human rights violations require coordinated efforts to combat effectively. Whistleblowers play a crucial role in exposing such challenges, and international collaboration enhances the impact of their contributions.

4. ***Avoiding Jurisdictional Arbitrage:***

   Whistleblowers may strategically choose where to report misconduct based on the strength of whistleblower protection laws in different jurisdictions. International collaboration helps prevent forum shopping, ensuring that individuals choose reporting avenues based on the nature of the misconduct rather than the level of legal protection.

5. ***Extraterritorial Application of Laws:***

   Extraterritorial Reach of Misconduct: Some acts of misconduct may have extraterritorial implications, affecting the interests of multiple countries. Collaboration facilitates the extraterritorial application of laws to hold wrongdoers accountable.

   Coordinated Legal Responses: When misconduct spans multiple jurisdictions, legal responses need to be coordinated to ensure a comprehensive and effective approach. Collaborative efforts help synchronize investigations, legal actions, and enforcement measures.

6. ***Strengthening Global Accountability:***

   Collaboration enhances the ability to promote accountability and transparency on a global scale. Coordinated efforts increase the likelihood that those responsible for misconduct are held accountable, contributing to a more just and ethical global environment.

7. ***Sharing Best Practices:***

   Different countries may have unique approaches to whistleblower protection that prove successful. International collaboration enables the sharing of best practices, allowing countries to learn from each other's experiences and improve their own whistleblower protection mechanisms.

8. ***Protection of Global Workforce:***

   Many individuals work for multinational companies or organizations with a presence in multiple countries. Collaborative efforts ensure that these employees, regardless of their location, have access to robust whistleblower protection.

9. ***Global Advocacy and Awareness:***

   Advocacy for Global Standards: Collaborative initiatives can advocate for the establishment of global standards for whistleblower protection. Global advocacy contributes to the development of a shared understanding of the importance of protecting whistleblowers.

   Raising Awareness: International collaboration helps raise awareness about the significance of whistleblowing in combating corruption, promoting integrity, and advancing ethical business practices. Collective efforts can contribute to a cultural shift that values and protects whistleblowers.

Final Thoughts

"In 'Beyond Checkboxes: The Human Element of GRC,' we embarked on a journey to explore the intricate intersections of Governance, Risk Management, and Compliance (GRC) through a lens that prioritizes the human element. This book delves into the critical chapters that underscore the importance of user-friendly security policies, the transformative potential of human-centric designs, and the evolving landscape of GRC in our increasingly interconnected world.

Beginning with the foundational understanding of the importance of user-friendly security policies, we uncovered the nuanced challenges of traditional, complex policy structures. The book then delved into the common misconceptions users hold about security, examining the impact of jargon on comprehension and advocating passionately for plain language in policy writing. As GRC experts, we explored the value of user input in policy creation, offering practical methods for collecting and implementing feedback.

Recognizing that tailoring policies to individual roles is paramount, the book explored options for customizable security settings and ways to accommodate the diverse needs of users. Visual aids were championed as tools to enhance policy comprehension, accompanied by real-world examples illustrating successful implementations of human-centric security policies.

Transitioning into the realm of training versus culture, we navigated the complexities of building a sustainable cybersecurity mindset. Definitions and discussions surrounding the significance of cybersecurity culture, the training versus culture dilemma, and the multifaceted aspects of cybersecurity education were explored in detail. Strategies for integrating training into daily operations, overcoming resistance to change, and evolving training methods and technologies were highlighted, with an eye toward future trends in cybersecurity education.

The book then shifted its focus to insider threats, recognizing and mitigating human risk from within. Comprehensive discussions encompassed the definition of insider threats, the human factor in cybersecurity, motivations behind insider threats, recognizing behavioral indicators, and risk factors associated with insider threats. Real-world case studies provided tangible examples of notable incidents, while behavioral analytics and anomaly detection emerged as vital tools for detection and prevention.

The final chapters underscored the pivotal role of leadership in GRC, examining how executives shape human behavior within organizations. Motivational factors driving employee compliance or resistance were explored, leading to an analysis of the concept of whistleblowing—a crucial component for encouraging reporting and continuous improvement.

In closing, we've traversed the landscapes of governance, risk management, and compliance, emphasizing the centrality of the human element. As we conclude this journey, we stand at the intersection of technology, ethics, and human behavior, understanding that the future of GRC relies on our collective commitment to fostering a culture of transparency, accountability, and innovation. 'Beyond Checkboxes' is not just a book—it's a call to action, urging organizations to embrace the human side of GRC for a more secure, resilient, and ethical future."

REFERENCE

"2011 UBS Rogue Trader Scandal." Wikipedia, 24 Oct. 2020, en.wikipedia.org/wiki/2011_UBS_rogue_trader_scandal.

"2017 Equifax Data Breach." Wikipedia, 2 Aug. 2020, en.wikipedia.org/wiki/2017_Equifax_data_breach. Accessed 10 Nov. 2023.

Benis, Michael. "The TJX Hack: A Case Study in Retail Cybersecurity." Www.linkedin.com, 22 Jan. 2023, www.linkedin.com/pulse/tjx-hack-case-study-retail-cybersecurity-michael-benis. Accessed 16 Nov. 2023.

Brown, Schuyler . "3 Types of Access Control: IT Security Models Explained | StrongDM." Discover.strongdm.com, 2023, www.strongdm.com/blog/types-of-access-control. Accessed 10 Nov. 2023.

Capital One. "2019 Capital One Cyber Incident | What Happened." Capital One, 23 Sept. 2019, www.capitalone.com/digital/facts2019/.

Carpenter, Perry. "Council Post: Five Cognitive Biases That Can Threaten Your Cybersecurity Efforts." Forbes, www.forbes.com/sites/forbesbusinesscouncil/2021/12/30/five-cognitive-biases-that-can-threaten-your-cybersecurity-efforts/?sh=268f3a2a9e31. Accessed 16 Nov. 2023.

Cuff, Benjamin M.P. , et al. Empathy: A Review of the Concept. Online, 2014, file:///C:/Users/HP/Downloads/Cuffetal2015EmpathyAReviewoftheConceptPrePrint2014.pdf. Accessed 16 Nov. 2023.

"ESG Controversies." Volkswagen Group, 18 July 2023, www.volkswagen-group.com/en/esg-controversies-15846.

"Gartner Identifies the Top Cybersecurity Trends for 2023." Gartner, www.gartner.com/en/newsroom/press-releases/04-12-2023-gartner-identifies-the-top-cybersecurity-trends-for-2023. Accessed 14 Nov. 2023.

Groome, David. An Introduction to Cognitive Psychology : Processes and Disorders. London Psychology Press, 2004.

"Harold T. Martin." Wikipedia, 27 Sept. 2023, en.wikipedia.org/wiki/Harold_T._Martin. Accessed 16 Nov. 2023.

Mitnick, Kevi, and William L. Simon. A Legendás Hacker. 2006.

Newcomb, Alyssa. "A Timeline of Facebook's Privacy Issues — and Its Responses." NBC News, 24 Mar. 2018, www.nbcnews.com/tech/social-media/timeline-facebook-s-privacy-issues-its-responses-n859651.

Ollmann, Gunter. The Phishing Guide Understanding & Preventing Phishing Attacks. June 2004.

Perell, David. "Why Did the Boeing 737 Max Crash? - David Perell." David Perell, 17 Dec. 2020, perell.com/essay/boeing-737-max/.

Rudolph, Manuel. User-Friendly and Tailored Policy Administration Points.

Segal, Troy. "Enron Scandal: The Fall of a Wall Street Darling ." Investopedia, 5 Apr. 2023, www.investopedia.com/updates/enron-scandal-summary/.

"SolarWinds." Wikipedia, 19 Aug. 2020, en.wikipedia.org/wiki/SolarWinds.

Wikipedia. "2020 Twitter Account Hijacking." Wikipedia, 2 Apr. 2021, en.wikipedia.org/wiki/2020_Twitter_account_hijacking.

"Wells Fargo Cross-Selling Scandal." Wikipedia, 18 Nov. 2022, en.wikipedia.org/wiki/Wells_Fargo_cross-selling_scandal.

Wikipedia Contributors. "2009–2011 Toyota Vehicle Recalls." Wikipedia, Wikimedia Foundation, 29 Oct. 2021, en.wikipedia.org/wiki/2009%E2%80%932011_Toyota_vehicle_recalls.

"Chelsea Manning." Wikipedia, Wikimedia Foundation, 19 Sept. 2019, en.wikipedia.org/wiki/Chelsea_Manning. Accessed Nov. 2023.

"Edward Snowden." Wikipedia, Wikimedia Foundation, 16 Mar. 2019, en.wikipedia.org/wiki/Edward_Snowden. Accessed 12 Nov. 2023.

"Volkswagen Emissions Scandal." Wikipedia, Wikimedia Foundation, 18 Mar. 2019, en.wikipedia.org/wiki/Volkswagen_emissions_scandal.

"WannaCry Ransomware Attack." Wikipedia, Wikimedia Foundation, 6 May 2019, en.wikipedia.org/wiki/WannaCry_ransomware_attack. Accessed 9 2023.

About The Author

The Author, Tolulope Michael, is a proud Computer Science graduate from the esteemed and prestigious Lagos State University. His love for technology, combined with a strong interest in cybersecurity, has driven him to dedicate close to two decades of his life to this field.

Over the years, he has gained valuable experience in various domains of cybersecurity, including Penetration Testing, Application Security Engineering, Cloud Security Engineering, and Governance, Risk and Compliance (GRC). He is proud to say that he has contributed to the growth of the industry, leaving a lasting impact with his expertise and knowledge.

In his quest to help others succeed in cybersecurity, he created ExcelMindCyber, a platform designed to provide comprehensive education in this field. His flagship program, "The Ultimate Cybersecurity Program" has already made a significant impact, helping many individuals realize their potential and earn multiple six figures.

He is grateful for the opportunity to share his passion and knowledge with others, and it brings him immense joy to see his students find success and fulfillment in this field. His journey in cybersecurity has been a rewarding one, and he is proud to be a part of this industry.He hopes to continue making a difference in the lives of those who share his love for cybersecurity, and is committed to helping them achieve their goals. This is his story, and he is proud to tell it.

With a clear and accessible writing style, he provides a roadmap for individuals looking to break into the field of cybersecurity, offering practical advice and actionable tips that will help you succeed in your journey. Whether you're a student, a professional looking for a change, or simply someone with an interest in cybersecurity, the author's insights and guidance will help you build the foundation you need for an exciting and rewarding career.